A Journey Through Time:

The Book of the Unknown, The Book of Echoes, and The Enchanted Spectacles

The Origin of
The Loveday Method®
A Trilogy
by
Geoffrey Loveday

A Journey Through Time

The Book of the Unknown, The Book of Echoes, and The Enchanted Spectacles

Author: Geoffrey Loveday

Copyright © 2025 by Geoffrey Loveday. All rights reserved.

The right of Geoffrey Loveday to be identified as the author of this work has been asserted in accordance with sections 77 and 78 of the Copyright, Designs, and Patents Act 1988.

First published in 2025
ISBN 978-1-917978-09-5 (Paperback)
ISBN 978-1-917978-10-1 (Hardback)
ISBN 978-1-917978-11-8 (E-Book)

Book cover design and layout by Geoffrey Loveday

Published by: Mindlayers Publishing

Mindlayers Publishing

35-37 Ludgate Hill,

London, England,

EC4M 7JN

Website: www.liverpoolhypnosis.co.uk

This book is intended for informational and entertainment purposes only. The author and publisher cannot be held responsible for any consequences arising from the usage of the information contained within this book. Neither the author nor the publisher assumes any responsibility or liability for how the contents are used.

A CIP (Cataloguing in Publication) record for this title is available from the British Library.

All Rights Reserved.

No part of this book may be reproduced, distributed, or transmitted in any form or by any means, electronic or mechanical, including photocopying, recording, or by any information storage or retrieval system, without the prior written permission of the author.

This novel is a work of fiction. Any resemblance to actual persons, living or dead, events, or locations is purely coincidental. The views expressed by the fictional characters do not necessarily reflect those of the author.

I wonder where life will take us now ...

And so the journey begins.

Let me take you on this magical adventure.

Contents

The Story Behind the Words 13

Dedication 16

Inspiration 20

Where Reality Meets Fantasy 23

The Book of the Unknown, The Book of Echoes, and The Enchanted Spectacles 24

    A Trilogy Bound Together 24

    The Book of the Unknown 25

    The Book of Echoes 26

    The Enchanted Spectacles 27

    A Journey Unseen, A World Unknown 29

The Book of the Unknown 31

    Chapter 1: The Cure for Life, A future World 31

    The Story of the Ancient One: The Writer of the Sacred Books 31

    Chapter 2: The Loveday Method 39

        Unlocking the Future and Revealing the Secrets of Ancient Books 39

    Chapter 3: Unlocking the Future 43

        A World Where Healing Knows No Limits 43

        The Loveday Method: From Past to Future 47

    Chapter 4: The Story of Kael: 52

        The Creator of The Book of the Unknown and the Reincarnation of Geoffrey Loveday 52

Chapter 5: The Stories You Are About to Read 63

   Truth or Fiction? The choice is yours 63

   Susanna and the Book of the Unknown: A Journey Into the Future 65

Chapter 6: The Manuscript 74

   The Book of the Unknown. 74

Chapter 7: Aelfric and the Book of the Unknown 84

   A Journey to the Future 84

Chapter 8: Nicholas and the Book of the Unknown 91

   A Journey of Loss and Healing 91

Chapter 9: Zasa's Awakening 99

   The Truth of Who He Really Was 99

Chapter 10: Final Chapter 106

   Or Is It Just the Beginning? 106

The Book of Echoes 111

The Legend of the Mystical Book: 111

   Breaking the Cycle: 111

      Chapter One: Whispers in the Dark 113

      Chapter Two: The Ink of Time 114

      Chapter Three: The First Life 115

      Chapter Four: The Wound beneath the Skin 118

      Chapter Five: Awakening 120

      Chapter Six: The Next Passage 121

      Chapter Seven: The Physician's Hands 122

      Chapter Eight: The Others Who Follow 124

      Epilogue: The First Seeker 125

The Loveday Method and the Seekers of Time 126

Chapter Nine: The First Seeker's Descent 126

Chapter Ten: A Life in the Water 127

Chapter Eleven: The Release 129

Chapter Twelve: The Others Who Come 130

Chapter Thirteen: The Guardian of the Book 131

Origins of the Book & the Web of Journeys 133

Chapter Fourteen: The First Scribe 133

Chapter Fifteen: The Birth of the Book 134

Chapter Sixteen: The Threads of Many Lives 136

Epilogue: The Next Guardian 137

The Echoes of Sir Roland 143

Echoes in the Present 147

A New Purpose 149

Echoes of Healing 150

The Healer's Burden 151

A Path Forward 153

Echoes That Heal 154

The Third Seeker: A Leader's Doubt 155

The Chief's Trial 156

Returning With Clarity 159

The Fourth Seeker: An Artist's Block 161

The Artisan's Rebellion 162

The Canvas Speaks Again 163

The Book of Echoes Finds Another Way 166

Chapter Seventeen: The Forgotten Name 166

Chapter Eighteen: The Bookshop on Fleet Street 167

Chapter Nineteen: A Life Once Lived 169

Chapter Twenty: The Buried Past............................ 170

Chapter Twenty-One: The Guardian's Choice 171

A New Seeker; A Different Time........ 174

    Chapter Twenty-Two: The Astronaut and the Book. 174

    Chapter Twenty-Three: The Artifact............... 175

    Chapter Twenty-Four: The Fall Through Memory ... 176

    Chapter Twenty-Five: The Soldier He Once Was 177

    Chapter Twenty-Six: The Choice That Was Never Made
.... 179

    Chapter Twenty-Seven: The Awakening................... 180

    Epilogue: The Next Guardian.................... 181

Another Seeker, Another Time 183

    Chapter Twenty-Eight: The Samurai and the Book . 183

    Chapter Twenty-Nine: The Warrior She Once Was.. 184

    Chapter Thirty: The Last Stand............................... 185

    Chapter Thirty-One: Breaking the Cycle 186

    Chapter Thirty-Two: The Return 187

    Chapter Thirty-Three: The Path of the Book............ 188

A New Seeker in the Industrial Age 190

    Chapter Thirty-Four: The Engineer and the Book ... 190

    Chapter Thirty-Five: The Weaver's Tale................... 191

    Chapter Thirty-Six: Embracing Transformation 192

    Epilogue: The Ever-Turning Wheel........................... 193

A New Seeker in the Digital Revolution 194

    Chapter Thirty-seven: The Programmer and the Book
.... 194

Chapter Thirty-eight: The Telegraph Operator's Dilemma 195

Chapter Thirty-nine: Embracing Change 196

Epilogue: The Ever-Turning Wheel 197

Chapter forty: The Spy and the Book 197

Chapter Forty-One: A Life He Shouldn't Remember 198

Chapter Forty-Two: The Guillotine's Shadow 199

Chapter Forty-Three: The Message Across Time 200

Chapter Forty-Four: The Spy's Next Move 201

Julian's Race Against Time 203

Chapter Forty-Five: The Web of Deceit 203

Chapter Forty-Six: The Confrontation 204

Chapter Forty-Seven: The Revelation 205

Chapter Forty-Eight: The Aftermath 206

A New Seeker in the Age of Exploration 208

Chapter Forty-Nine: The Navigator and the Book ... 208

Chapter Fifty: The Viking's Voyage 209

Chapter Fifty-One: The Return 210

Chapter Fifty-Two: The Philosopher's Revelation 211

Chapter Fifty-Three The Alchemist's Journey 212

Chapter Fifty-four: The Enlightened Path 213

Chapter Fifty-Five: The Patriot's Awakening 214

Chapter Fifty-Six: The Spartan's Trial 215

Chapter Fifty-Seven: The Midnight Ride 216

Chapter Fifty-Eight: The Guardian's Revelation 218

Chapter Fifty-Nine: The Awakening 219

Chapter Sixty: The Ancestral Memory 220

Chapter Sixty-One: The Revelation 221
A Meeting Across Time 223
    Chapter Sixty-Two: The Convergence 223
    Chapter Sixty-Three the Dialogue Beyond Time 223
    Chapter Sixty-Four: The Parting Gift 225
The Book of Echoes, ... 227
    Ancient Mystical Book 228
This Is Just the Beginning 231
Beyond Time: The Power to Revisit, Rewrite, and Heal
.... 233
The Enchanted Spectacles 235
    Chapter One: The Book of Echoes 237
    Chapter Two: Remembering the Spectacles 241
    Chapter Three: Through the Veil 249
    Chapter Four: The Girl Who Remembered Fire 252
    Chapter Five: The Boy Who Dreamed in Futures 258
    Chapter Six: The Woman Who Carried the Ache 262
    Chapter Seven: The Child Who Spoke in Stars 266
    Chapter Eight: The Man Who Remembered at the End
.... 272
    Chapter Nine: The Woman Who Tried to Forget 277
    Chapter Ten: The First Remembering 282
    Chapter Eleven: The One Who Saw Through the Flame
.... 286
    Chapter Twelve: The Man Who Fell Through the Sky. 291
    Chapter Thirteen: The One Who Didn't Believe 295
    Chapter Fourteen: The Great Return 300

Chapter 15: The Sorrow in the Air 304

Chapter Sixteen: The Girl Who Couldn't Breathe 308

Chapter Seventeen: The Seamstress of Silence 312

Chapter Eighteen: The Soldier Who Never Spoke 317

Chapter Nineteen: The One Who Almost Missed It 322

A Soul Letter 326

Chapter Twenty: The Thread of Time 328

The Book of the Unknown, The Book of Echoes, The
Enchanted Spectacles: What Is Real? 333

The Story Behind the Words

My name is Geoffrey Loveday, and like you, I walk a journey shaped by learning, healing, and a constant pursuit to make sense of it all.

Yes, I've written eleven books and earned various professional credentials along the way. But none of those titles truly define me. What truly drives me is something much deeper—a quiet, relentless pull to write, to share, to create.

I can't always pinpoint where this call comes from, but I know it's ancient, persistent, and alive in every fiber of my being.

I don't write because I have all the answers. I write because there's a knowing inside me that the truth we all seek is worth sharing. That real healing begins when we embrace honesty. That when we share our stories with authenticity, we begin to reconnect—with ourselves, and with one another.

My work is not about fixing what's broken in others; it's about guiding people back to who they truly are—beneath the layers of inherited wounds, past conditioning, and hidden pain.

Through The Loveday Method and Inherited Therapy, I offer paths to healing, not as someone with all the answers, but as a fellow traveler who has learned how to begin again.

As a certified hypnoanalyst, clinical hypnotherapy instructor, and guide to thousands of transformative journeys, I've witnessed profound change—not through force, but through the gentle process of remembering.

The true magic happens when people rediscover their own truth and power, and in doing so, come home to themselves.

I don't see myself as anything extraordinary. But I know, without question, that what I've been given is meant to be shared.

This is my gift to you, offered with the hope that it may reach those who need it the most.

Dedication

This book is an offering of love and gratitude to the incredible souls whose strength, wisdom, and unwavering love have shaped me in ways words can barely express. Your influence runs through me, etched deeply into who I am. The impact you've made on my life—profound, sacred, and lasting—continues to guide me through every step of this journey.

To my father—your steady presence and the love you gave without condition still resonate in every part of my life. Though I can no longer hear your voice, your guidance whispers in every decision I make, your strength steadying me through every challenge. In the quiet space you left, I've come to understand the power of a love that endures beyond time—a love that still anchors me when everything else feels uncertain.

To my mother—our time together was brief, but your light still shines brightly within me. You showed me the delicate beauty of life, teaching me the strength to hold tight to the things that matter most. In every act of tenderness, I feel your spirit close, guiding me in every quiet moment.

To my grandparents, aunts, and uncles—your stories are woven into the fabric of who I am. You gave me roots and a sense of belonging, gifting me a legacy of kindness and grace that I carry with me always. Your love was the first safe place I knew, and it remains a steady foundation under my feet.

To my uncles and aunts—thank you for taking me in when I was young and nurturing me with your boundless care. You shaped me into who I am today, and your love continues to guide me in all I do.

To Alma and Leon, my in-laws—your open arms and generous hearts have made me feel part of something greater than myself. The love you shared with me has enriched my life in ways I never thought possible. Your quiet kindness will forever be a part of my soul.

To my beloved wife—though you are no longer physically with me, your love still shapes the world around me. I see you in the laughter of our children, in the quiet mornings, in the quiet strength you left behind. Your faith in me continues to drive everything I do, and your presence is still felt in every word I write. You will always be a part of me, a part of everything I am and will become.

To our children—your hearts are my greatest gift, my constant inspiration, and my strength. You've shown me that love endures, grows, and flourishes, even in the face of life's toughest challenges. In your love, I find the endless promise of goodness in the world.

To my grandchildren—your joy is a light that fills my life, your innocence a reminder that hope is always within reach. You carry forward the love and spirit of those who came before you, and through you, I see a future filled with endless possibilities.

To my sons-in-law—thank you for joining our family, not only by name but by spirit. Your strength, kindness, and respect have added to the richness of this circle we hold close.

To my brothers—though your absence leaves a quiet ache in my heart, your memory remains a constant well of strength. I still hear your laughter in my mind, feel the pride you held for me in my soul. You are still with me, in every breath, every step I take forward.

To my dear friends, mentors, and companions on this journey—your belief in me has been a constant source of support. Your love, wisdom, and presence have carried me through both the darkest and brightest moments. Without you, I would not be here today.

This book is for all of you. Every word is touched by your love, your courage, your influence. You are the heartbeat behind these pages, the reason they exist. From the deepest part of my being, thank you—for standing by me, for lifting me up, for loving me. Always.

Inspiration

This book is a heartfelt tribute to the incredible resilience of those who face illness with unwavering courage, grace, and determination. Whether you're in the midst of the battle, healing, or still navigating your path—this is for you. Your strength has touched my soul in ways words can't capture, and your stories continue to inspire countless others, showing us all the true meaning of perseverance.

To those who have shared their journeys with such openness: thank you. In your vulnerability, you've shown us that strength isn't just about fighting—it's about enduring, adapting, and growing in life's most uncertain and difficult moments.

To the healthcare professionals and researchers: your dedication to healing and discovery is a beacon of hope. You don't just treat the illness; you nurture the spirit, offering new possibilities where there once seemed to be none. Your work changes lives in ways that can't always be seen, but are felt deeply.

To the families, caregivers, and loved ones who stand by those in need: your love, your patience, your quiet strength are profound acts of care. You give more than support—you give hope, peace, and a reminder of the human connection that sustains us all. Your presence has not only touched this book but also my heart, deeply.

To the organizations and foundations that tirelessly advocate, educate, and uplift: your work is a lifeline. You bring hope to the forgotten, light to the darkest corners, and the promise of a better tomorrow. The impact of your efforts goes beyond statistics—it is felt in the lives of the people you touch.

To my readers: your willingness to embrace these stories with empathy and an open heart creates a bridge for understanding and healing. By reading, listening, and sharing, you help build a community of care, where healing can truly begin.

And to those who supported me in creating this work—my mentors, editors, and those who believed in this project from the very start: thank you. Your encouragement, guidance, and belief in this journey have made all the difference.

This book is more than words on a page. It is a celebration of human strength, the boundless capacity for love, and the enduring will to rise again. Thank you for being part of this shared story.

Where Reality Meets Fantasy

This book is more than mere words on a page; it's a portal, a gateway through time and possibility. Within these pages, you won't just read stories; you will live them. These journeys aren't confined to fiction; they pulse with truth, waiting to unfold in the depths of your imagination. Every adventure, every revelation, is as real as you choose to make it.

You can travel anywhere; across distant worlds, through forgotten histories, or into the deepest corners of the human soul. The only limit is your belief. Trust in yourself, open your mind, and step beyond the ordinary.

Let the impossible become real.

The Book of the Unknown, The Book of Echoes, and The Enchanted Spectacles

A Trilogy Bound Together

There exists a book—an ancient and sacred text—so powerful, so mysterious, that it is said to contain the very essence of existence.

This book is not merely ink on paper, but a gateway, a portal that binds together the Book of the Unknown, the Book of Echoes, and the Enchanted Spectacles into a single, living manuscript.

Each section of the book holds secrets of a world unseen and a journey unknown, a truth that has been hidden for eons and awaits those brave enough to unlock its power.

The Book of the Unknown

The first section of the book, the Book of the Unknown, is a guide to a future where all suffering, disease, and pain have been erased. It is a vision of a world free from the dark shadows that plague mankind—where healing is a natural part of life, where the mind, body, and soul exist in perfect harmony, and where the human race lives in balance with the earth.

This book is not a work of prophecy, but a blueprint—a map of what can be. The Book of the Unknown contains visions of a world we cannot yet fully comprehend, a world of possibility, of growth, and of unimaginable peace.

It shows us that healing is not an impossible dream but a destiny waiting to unfold. The wisdom within the pages speaks of a time when humanity has unlocked the deepest mysteries of existence, and we will have conquered the diseases of the mind and body.

The Book of the Unknown gives a glimpse of the future, but it is more than just a dream of what is to come—it is a reminder that this world of healing is within our reach. The key lies in our collective will to awaken to the truth of who we are and what we are capable of.

The Book of Echoes

The second section of the book, the Book of Echoes, is a record of the past—a tapestry of memories, lives, and stories that have reverberated through time, shaping the world as we know it. It is a reflection of all that has come before, the whispers of those who have lived, loved, and suffered.

The Book of Echoes captures the essence of the human experience, revealing the patterns and lessons of our ancestors.

Each page of the Book of Echoes tells the story of a soul who has walked before, their journey leaving a mark on the fabric of time. The book does not merely recount history; it captures the energy, the emotions, and the wisdom of those who have lived.

In the Book of Echoes, we hear the voices of the past, their fears, their joys, their triumphs and losses, and we feel the ripple of their actions across generations.

But the Book of Echoes is not just a reminder of what has been—it is a bridge. It connects us to the past so that we may heal the wounds of yesterday and build a future founded on the lessons we have learned.

The echoes of those who have come before us shape the path we walk today, and in their wisdom, we find the strength to move forward.

The Enchanted Spectacles

The third and final section of the book, the Enchanted Spectacles, is a vision of the spiritual realm, a place where the soul is free to explore and transcend the limitations of the physical world.

The Enchanted Spectacles is not a mere dream or vision, but a deep spiritual awakening, a shift in consciousness that allows us to see beyond the veil of reality and witness the hidden energies that bind all things together.

This section of the book is a realm of mysticism and magic, where the boundaries between the physical and spiritual worlds dissolve. In the Enchanted Spectacles, we are shown the true interconnectedness of all life—how every action, every thought, every emotion ripples through the fabric of existence, affecting everything around it.

It is a place where the soul is free to soar, where the power of love, compassion, and understanding can heal not just the individual, but the world itself.

The Enchanted Spectacles teaches us that healing is not just about the body or the mind; it is about the soul. It is about understanding that we are all part of something greater, a universal flow of energy that connects all beings.

Through this understanding, we can transcend our limitations, awaken to our true potential, and become the healers we were always meant to be.

A Journey Unseen, A World Unknown

Bound together within the pages of this single, living manuscript, the Book of the Unknown, the Book of Echoes, and the Enchanted Spectacles form a trilogy that holds the keys to unlocking the greatest mysteries of existence. Each section reveals a different layer of reality—a world unseen, a journey unknown—but together, they offer a roadmap for humanity's future.

Through the Book of the Unknown, we are shown the possibility of a healed world, one free from suffering and disease. Through the Book of Echoes, we are reminded of the wisdom and lessons of the past, the wisdom that shapes our present and guides us toward a brighter future.

And through the Enchanted Spectacles, we are awakened to the spiritual realm, where healing is not just a physical act, but a deep, soul-nourishing journey.

The journey of the Book of the Unknown is not just about finding the future—it is about discovering the power within ourselves to create it. The Book of Echoes shows us that our actions, our choices, and our love leave an imprint on the world, shaping the lives of those who come after us.

And the Enchanted Spectacles teaches us that healing comes not only from what we do, but from who we are, from our deepest spiritual connection to the world and to each other.

The trilogy that lies within these pages is not just a book—it is a call to action. It is a reminder that we are the architects of our own future, that healing begins with us, and that the world we seek is within our grasp.

The Book of the Unknown, the Book of Echoes, and the Enchanted Spectacles are not just stories or ancient texts—they are the truth, waiting to be uncovered, waiting for humanity to awaken to the power of healing, peace, and love.

The question now remains: Will we listen to the call of the trilogy and step into the future that awaits us? Only time will tell. But the journey has already begun.

The Book of the Unknown

Chapter 1: The Cure for Life, A future World

The Story of the Ancient One: The Writer of the Sacred Books

Long ago, before time as we understand it began, there lived an ancient figure known as *Talinor*, a being whose wisdom surpassed the bounds of human comprehension. Talinor was not born in the conventional way, nor was he a man in the sense we know. He existed as a being of light and consciousness, far ahead of the mortal realm. His spirit roamed across the ages, from the dawn of creation to the far future, observing, learning, and recording the cycles of life, death, and transformation.

Talinor, the ancient scribe, had a vision—one that stretched far beyond the world he inhabited. He saw a time when humanity, in its early stages, would be plagued by suffering and disease. He saw people held captive by their own minds and bodies, burdened by inherited trauma, mental illness, and physical ailments. And yet, in his vision, he also saw a future—a time when all of this would be healed, when the human race would overcome the challenges that had bound them for so long. This future was not just one of survival, but one of thriving in complete health, peace, and unity.

Talinor knew that this future healing was possible, but he also understood that humanity needed guidance. The wisdom required to transcend the suffering of their time would not come overnight. It would take centuries—perhaps millennia—before the world was ready to embrace it. And so, Talinor began his work. He created three sacred texts, each written with the intention of preparing humanity for the time when they would be ready to awaken to this future. These books were not simply pieces of knowledge; they were seeds, planted deep in the consciousness of humanity, waiting to be discovered when the time was right.

The first book, *The Book of the Unknown*, was written with the vision of the future at its core. Talinor foresaw a time when mankind would have unlocked the secrets to healing every disease, both physical and mental. A time when suffering, as humanity knew it, would be a thing of the past. He wrote of this future with such clarity and detail that it was as if he had already stepped into it himself. He knew that mankind could not see this vision clearly yet, but he also knew that one day, a method would emerge that would allow the human mind to access it. This book was hidden away, encased in a crystal, to be revealed when humanity was ready to understand its full potential. It was a map for the future, a guide to the healing that was yet to come.

The second book, *The Book of Echoes*, was written to help humanity understand its past. Talinor knew that to heal, one had to understand the roots of their suffering. The echoes of past lives, past mistakes, and past wisdom needed to be heard. This book was a collection of the lessons learned from those who had walked before. It was not just a chronicle of history, but a guide to unlocking the wisdom of past generations— wisdom that would be crucial for overcoming the challenges of the present. Talinor knew that humanity needed to learn from its mistakes, but also that the lessons of the past were never truly gone. They echoed through time, waiting to be rediscovered.

The final book, *The Enchanted Spectacles*, was written with a deeper, spiritual wisdom. Talinor saw that healing was not just about physical health but about the harmony between the body, mind, and spirit. This book spoke of a time when humanity would come into alignment with the earth, when the physical and spiritual worlds would merge in perfect balance. It was a vision of enlightenment, a time when humanity would live not only in perfect health but in unity with the natural world. Talinor knew that to achieve this, mankind needed to awaken spiritually. The path to healing lay not just in medicine or technology but in understanding the interconnectedness of all life.

Talinor wrote these books not for his time, but for the future. He understood that humanity was not yet ready to comprehend the depth of his wisdom, and so, he hid them away. But his knowledge would not be lost. It would survive, tucked away in the recesses of time, waiting for the right moment to emerge.

Why did Talinor write these books? The answer lies in his deep love for humanity. Despite the suffering he saw, Talinor believed in the potential of the human spirit. He believed that if humanity could access the right wisdom and tools, they could transcend their limitations and reach their true potential. His love for mankind drove him to leave behind these sacred texts—keys to unlocking a future of peace, health, and spiritual enlightenment.

Talinor's work was not finished in his lifetime. His name would not be remembered in the history books, and his existence would fade into the mists of time. Yet, his impact would be felt for generations to come. The books he wrote, the wisdom he imparted, would guide humanity toward a future of complete healing. And the connection between Talinor's work and the *Loveday Method* is no coincidence. Through the Loveday Method, we are able to access not just our past traumas but the future that Talinor foresaw—a future of healing, wholeness, and unity.

Talinor, in his timeless wisdom, knew that humanity could not walk this path alone. He left behind these books as a guide, knowing that one day, when the time was right, humanity would discover them. And through the Loveday Method, we are now on the brink of that discovery. We are not just healing the past, but unlocking the future that Talinor envisioned for us.

The sacred texts were written with love and with the intention of guiding humanity to a place where they could thrive, free from the suffering that has plagued them for so long. And now, through the Loveday Method, we are finally beginning to see the future that Talinor saw so long ago—a future where healing is not just a dream, but a reality. The story of Talinor, the ancient scribe, is the story of all of us, as we journey toward the future of complete healing and awakening.

There exists a legend, an ancient and mysterious tale, of a book—The Book of the Unknown. No one knows where it originated from, or who first wrote its pages. Some say it was placed in a crystal, its secrets hidden away until the right moment. The book, when it appears, is not like any other. It does not merely tell stories of the past; it opens a doorway into the future—into a world where every disease, physical and mental, has been cured. It holds the key to unlocking a time when suffering, in all its forms, has been erased.

This book is said to have been written *before time itself,* its words etched into existence long before our minds could comprehend such concepts as disease, pain, or suffering. It is mystical, transcendent, and unlike anything that could be created by ordinary hands. The question is, who wrote it? And why?

The Book of the Unknown is more than just a legend—it's a mystery that beckons us to uncover its origins. Who was the author, and what wisdom did they possess to write of a future so advanced that all ailments are no longer part of the human experience? What is the true purpose of this book, and why is it revealed at this time in history, when mankind stands on the brink of extraordinary healing and transformation?

We need to find out. We need to bring the book back, uncover its secrets, and understand its origins. The future it holds promises a world where healing is not just possible, but a given. Imagine a future where no one suffers from disease, where mental health is nurtured and restored, and where every human being lives with vitality, peace, and balance.

But to unlock that future, we must first understand the story behind the book—its true author, the force that brought it into existence, and the reason it was written. What knowledge does it hold about our potential, about the path we are destined to walk? And what will happen when we finally learn its secrets?

The Book of the Unknown may hold the answers to the very healing we have long sought. It may guide us toward the future of perfect health, peace, and freedom. But to find the way, we must look beyond what we know, into the realms of mystery and possibility, and discover why this book was written—and who the true author is. The answers await, and they may change everything we thought we knew about healing, life, and the future of mankind.

Chapter 2: The Loveday Method

Unlocking the Future and Revealing the Secrets of Ancient Books

The Loveday Method has long been a powerful tool for healing the past—guiding individuals to uncover and release inherited trauma, emotional wounds, and past life experiences that still affect their present. Through this method, people have learned to confront the events that shaped their lives, and in doing so, they have found the freedom to heal and transform. But what if this method holds even greater potential? What if it could not only unlock the past but also offer a glimpse into the future—a future where all diseases, both physical and mental, have been healed and suffering is no more?

Imagine stepping into a time far beyond our own, a time when every illness, every condition, every mental struggle has been resolved. A time where mankind has discovered the cures for all that afflicts us—cancer, diabetes, heart disease, depression, and so much more.

Could it be that by tapping into this method, we could see this future, a world where complete healing is a reality? A future that transcends the pain and limitations of today, where humanity lives in harmony, free from suffering and disease?

This idea extends beyond healing the past. There are ancient books, such as *The Book of the Unknown*, *The Book of Echoes*, and *The Enchanted Spectacles*, that hold the keys to deeper mysteries—books that speak of times long before us, written by those whose wisdom we can barely comprehend. What if these texts hold the secrets to a future where all disease is eradicated? What if they contain knowledge about the very healing we seek, not just for ourselves but for all of mankind?

The *Book of the Unknown*, in particular, is shrouded in mystery. It is said to describe a future where all diseases have been cured and humanity is free from suffering. Who wrote this book, and why? Could it be that the knowledge it holds was written by beings who understood what is possible when humanity has unlocked the full potential of healing, or could it have been written by those who saw a time yet to come, when we would have the answers we desperately seek?

Then there is *The Book of Echoes*, believed to contain the whispers of past lives, reverberating memories and experiences that have left an imprint on the present. But what if these echoes also reach forward in time? What if they are not only memories of the past, but glimpses of a future where every ailment is healed? What if the echoes of that future are already calling us, guiding us towards a time of total well-being and peace?

The Enchanted Spectacles—a book that many believe holds secrets of the spiritual realms, where the soul journeys to find peace and healing. Could it be that this book, too, has knowledge of a time when the spiritual and physical realms are perfectly aligned? What if it describes a world where the healing of the body and mind is intertwined with the healing of the soul, creating a truly harmonious existence?

The question is: Can we use what we know to not only heal the past but also unlock the future? Can we journey forward through the pages of these mystical books, and discover the true story behind their creation? The answers are within our reach, but to find them, we must move beyond what we already know. We must tap into the potential of a future that holds the cures for all diseases, the healing of all suffering, and the balance of body, mind, and spirit.

If we can access the past and unravel its mysteries, why can't we do the same with the future? Why can't we step into a time when mankind has unlocked all the answers to our greatest challenges, when health is a given and suffering is no more?

The time has come to go beyond what we know, to step into a future where all things are possible, where healing is not just a possibility, but a given. The journey of discovery is not just about understanding the past, but about creating the future we desire—a future of complete health, peace, and spiritual alignment. The Loveday Method is our guide to that future. Let us begin the journey.

Chapter 3: Unlocking the Future

A World Where Healing Knows No Limits.

When Daniel came to see me in April 2025, he was trapped in the grip of a cocaine addiction. He had tried to break free before, but nothing seemed to work. He came to me with a heavy heart, desperate for a change but uncertain if it was even possible. Over the course of six sessions, we began to work together, delving into the depths of his subconscious, unravelling the layers of pain, fear, and addiction that had held him captive for so long.

In our third session, on 20th May 2025, I decided to take him on a journey unlike any he had experienced before. I asked him to imagine stepping into a future where he had already made the decision to stop using cocaine—a place where he was free, healthy, and whole. We went beyond just visualising the future; we took him to a time, a place, where the suffering from addiction no longer existed.

We entered what I call the Akashic Library of Life, a place where the story of every soul is written. A book appeared before Daniel—his own book of life. When he opened it, the page was blank. I asked him, "What does this mean to you?" His response was simple but profound: "A new beginning." I encouraged him to write down what he wanted, what he desired with all his heart. Whatever he wrote, I told him, would manifest.

And then, something magical happened. Daniel found himself in a future world. He was standing in a beautiful castle, surrounded by peace and health. He was with his wife, and together, they made a promise to each other: he would stop using cocaine. He saw everything so clearly—everything was exactly as he had imagined it. The stairs, the furniture, the warmth in the air. It felt real. He felt alive with hope, and for the first time, he believed that the life he envisioned could actually happen.

But when I spoke with Daniel in June 2025, just a few months later, he was still struggling with his addiction. Despite everything we had explored, despite the powerful vision of his future, he doubted whether it was possible for him to change. He still felt trapped by his old habits. He called me, apologising for not believing in the journey we had taken together. He wasn't ready to stop—not yet. But something inside him had shifted. That conversation was a turning point.

That weekend, Daniel and his wife took their first break away from their children in eight years. They went to a place that felt strikingly familiar to him—the very place he had seen in his vision. It was the same castle, the same peaceful surroundings, the same sense of health and freedom. As he stood there, surrounded by the love of his wife, Daniel realised that the future he had seen wasn't just a dream. It was real. It was waiting for him.

At that moment, something extraordinary happened. The addiction that had held him captive for so long lost its power. Daniel stopped. He couldn't believe it, but it was true. He had finally broken free. For the first time in years, he felt a sense of freedom he had never thought possible. He called me to thank me, but it wasn't just about gratitude—it was about the realisation that, through our work together, he had stepped into a future where anything was possible.

That moment made me wonder: What if it's not just about healing the past, but about stepping into a future where all things are possible? What if we could take people not just to a time of recovery, but to a future where every disease—physical and mental—had been cured? A future where suffering no longer existed, and mankind had unlocked the secrets to perfect health, peace, and well-being.

What if we could transcend time itself, not just go back to the past, but travel far into the future—a future where diseases like cancer, diabetes, and heart disease are no longer part of our reality? A future where mental health issues are healed, and the pain of addiction, trauma, and suffering is wiped away. Could it be possible for mankind to find a way to heal the physical, emotional, and mental wounds that we've created over centuries?

What if this journey we took with Daniel was just the beginning? What if *The Loveday Method* could evolve into something even greater—a tool that allows people to step into a world where they are not just healed, but truly whole, at peace, and free from the suffering that has plagued mankind for so long?

Could we take people into a future where the impossible becomes possible? Where mankind has discovered the cures for every disease, where suffering is a thing of the past, and where we live in a world of complete harmony—physically, mentally, and emotionally?

The journey of life is just beginning. And if we can imagine a future like this, what else is possible? What could we unlock, what could we heal, if we are brave enough to dream beyond the limits of our current reality?

Let the journey of life begin—because if we dare to imagine it, perhaps we can bring that future to life.

The Loveday Method: From Past to Future

A Journey to a World without Disease and Suffering

By using the Loveday Method, we have the ability to guide individuals back in time, allowing them to relive a life before they were born, to unlock the deepest parts of their subconscious and heal from the past. But why stop there? If we can go back, why can't we venture forward into the future?

Imagine a time when all diseases—physical and mental—are no longer a burden. A time when mankind has found the cures for cancer, diabetes, heart disease, and all other afflictions that have plagued humanity for centuries. Why couldn't we travel to that future, where suffering is no more, and where people are truly healed, both inside and out?

The future holds limitless possibilities. Through the Loveday Method, we can not only understand the past but also explore a future where healing knows no boundaries, where pain and suffering have been entirely alleviated, and where mankind lives in harmony, free from disease. If we can relive our past, why not step into a future of complete peace, health, and freedom?

The question now is not whether we can travel to the future—but when we will.

The Loveday Method has already proven to be a powerful tool for unlocking the depths of the past, taking individuals back in time to relive moments before their birth, unearthing forgotten experiences, and healing wounds that have shaped their present reality. It has helped people discover and heal the roots of their struggles, allowing them to break free from old patterns of pain, fear, and limitation. But if we can access the past, why stop there? Why not stretch the boundaries of possibility and journey into a future where suffering, disease, and mental anguish are no longer a part of the human experience?

Imagine a future where illness is no more. A future where cancer, heart disease, diabetes, and mental health struggles have been eradicated—where science and the human spirit have united to find cures for every disease and end the suffering that mankind has endured for centuries. Imagine a time where people are no longer enslaved by the ailments of the body or mind. Healing is not just a hope, it is a reality. The future is not filled with hospitals, doctors, and treatments, but with vitality, freedom, and peace.

Why should we limit ourselves to reliving the past when we have the potential to unlock the future—a future that holds the answers to every ailment we have faced, a future where humanity is truly free from the shackles of disease and suffering? If the Loveday Method can take us back to before we were born to explore the roots of our troubles, why can't we also journey forward, deep into a time when healing is complete? A future where not only our bodies but also our minds and spirits are fully restored, balanced, and at peace?

Imagine stepping into that world—a world where every sickness is healed, where our minds are clear, strong, and free of the burdens that hold us back, where humanity lives in complete harmony with itself and the earth. Why can't we, through the Loveday Method, access that future and see what it looks like for ourselves? Why can't we step into a time where the limitations of our current existence no longer apply?

What if the future is waiting for us to step into it, to bring this vision of peace and health into our present reality? What if we can tap into that potential now, harnessing the power of the Loveday Method to shape a future free from suffering? If we can transform the past, why not the future?

The future is not a distant dream—it is a possibility, a reality waiting to be realised. And if we dare to journey there, perhaps we can begin to heal not only ourselves but the world. The question is not *whether* we can journey into the future—but when we will choose to make that leap, and what incredible healing we will discover along the way.

The time to begin is now. Let the journey into the future of limitless healing begin.

Chapter 4: The Story of Kael:

The Creator of The Book of the Unknown and the Reincarnation of Geoffrey Loveday

Long ago, in an age lost to time, there lived a being of profound wisdom and spiritual awareness named Kael. He was not like the mortals of his time—Kael was a soul of extraordinary consciousness, a being who could see beyond the limitations of the material world. Kael's understanding of existence was far beyond what any mortal could comprehend. He had a vision—a vision of a world where mankind could live free from suffering, a world where all diseases, physical and mental, had been eradicated.

Kael knew that for this future to come to fruition, humanity needed guidance—someone to show them the path. He set out to write a series of sacred texts, each filled with wisdom and knowledge, to be passed down through generations. His most important work was The Book of the Unknown, a sacred manuscript that depicted a world in which suffering, disease, and mental anguish were no more. A world where mankind existed in perfect health, peace, and harmony. This book was written not for his time, but for a future age, a time when humanity would be ready to receive its teachings.

Kael understood that his life would not witness the world he had envisioned, but he also knew that his soul's work was far from finished. He believed that his writing would plant the seeds of healing for future generations, which would only blossom once the world was ready. The Book of the Unknown was hidden away, not to be revealed until the right moment—a time when the human race had evolved enough to understand its profound wisdom.

As Kael's life came to an end, his works remained hidden in the sands of time, waiting for a future humanity to discover them. But Kael's mission was far from over. His spirit did not fade away—it was reborn into a new life, a new body, with the same purpose: to heal, guide, and awaken humanity. This soul, which had once been Kael, would reincarnate as Geoffrey Loveday—a man whose journey would lead him to discover the Loveday Method, a powerful tool for healing, which would ultimately unlock the ancient wisdom Kael had left behind.

In the year 2025, the Loveday Method, which was initially designed to help people heal their past traumas, began to take on a deeper purpose. People began to experience not only healing from their present struggles but also visions of a world that seemed impossibly peaceful and whole—images of the very future Kael had written about in The Book of the Unknown. Through the Loveday Method, individuals were accessing not just memories of past lives, but glimpses of the future—a future where all disease was cured, and humanity lived in perfect balance.

Geoffrey Loveday, who had long felt a deep connection to the art of healing, began to have vivid dreams, hearing voices and messages that seemed to come from another time. At first, he could not explain what he was experiencing, but gradually, he realised that these messages were not just random thoughts. They were the whispers of Kael's ancient wisdom, calling him to unlock the very books that had been written so long ago.

It soon became clear that Geoffrey Loveday was not merely using the Loveday Method to help others heal from past traumas. He was, in fact, reconnecting with the soul of Kael, the very being who had written the sacred texts. The Loveday Method was not just a tool for personal healing—it was the key to unlocking Kael's vision, a vision that had been passed down through time and now, through Geoffrey, would be realised.

Geoffrey's work began to reveal more than just individual healing. As he guided others through the Loveday Method, people started to experience the world Kael had written about—a world where healing was complete, and suffering was no more. They began to experience not just physical healing but spiritual awakenings as well. They saw themselves in a world where disease was a distant memory, where the human body, mind, and spirit existed in perfect harmony.

Geoffrey Loveday's awakening was no coincidence. His soul had once been Kael's, and now, through the Loveday Method, Geoffrey had come full circle. The method itself was part of Kael's design, a way to bring the healing knowledge of the past, present, and future together. Geoffrey had been reincarnated to complete the work Kael had started so long ago, and through him, the world was beginning to experience the future Kael had written into The Book of the Unknown.

The connection between Kael and Geoffrey Loveday was not merely one of wisdom—it was a deeper, spiritual connection. It was as though Kael had consciously chosen to reincarnate at this critical moment in history, when humanity was finally ready to unlock the healing that had been written for them. Geoffrey, in his soul's journey, was simply the vessel through which Kael's work would come to fruition.

As more individuals worked with the Loveday Method, they, too, began to access the ancient wisdom hidden within Kael's books. The Book of the Unknown was no longer a distant prophecy; it was becoming a living reality. The world that Kael had once seen in his visions was now beginning to emerge. Through the method, people were healing not just physically, but on a spiritual and emotional level, connecting with a future where suffering was no more.

The time had come for Kael's mission to be realised. His soul's journey, from his original life as Kael to his reincarnation as Geoffrey Loveday, had been leading to this moment. Geoffrey was the key to unlocking the sacred knowledge Kael had left behind, and the Loveday Method was the tool that would bring Kael's vision of healing and peace into the world.

Through the Loveday Method, humanity began to access The Book of the Unknown, The Book of Echoes, and the wisdom of The Enchanted Spectacles. These texts, written by Kael, were no longer just words on a page—they were becoming a guide for a new world, one in which complete healing was possible. The world Kael had envisioned was now within reach, and Geoffrey Loveday had become the vessel through which this ancient knowledge would be passed on.

The story of Kael, the ancient scribe, and Geoffrey Loveday, his reincarnated self, is not just one of personal healing. It is the story of humanity's awakening to the truth of their potential—a truth that was written long ago, waiting for the right time to be discovered. That time is now. The Loveday Method is the key, and the future that Kael had foreseen is beginning to unfold before us. The journey of healing is no longer a distant dream—it is becoming our reality.

The Book of the Unknown was never meant to be seen by the eyes of humanity until the time was right. It was not placed in a library, nor was it a physical object that could be touched or studied. Its essence transcended the physical realm, and it had to be hidden in a place that no one would ever think to look. It was not merely a book of knowledge—it was a key, a guide to the healing of the world, a world that was yet to come.

Kael, a being far beyond mortal understanding, knew that humanity would not be ready for this book in his time. The healing it offered, the knowledge it contained, was far too advanced, far too powerful for the world as it existed. So, he took it upon himself to ensure that the book would survive the force of time and remain hidden until the world was ready to unlock its secrets. The Book of the Unknown had to be preserved, and Kael knew that the best way to safeguard it was not through conventional means.

Thus, the book was hidden within the depths of a magical crystal—an object of immense power, invisible to the untrained eye. No one would ever suspect the crystal, and even if they did, it would remain elusive, out of reach. The crystal was not just a vessel—it was a barrier, protecting the Book of the Unknown from the ravages of time, and only one person would be able to unlock its secrets: Kael himself, when he was reborn.

The power of the Book of the Unknown was tied to Kael's soul. The book's hidden location was etched into the fabric of his consciousness, buried deep within the memories of every life he had ever lived. But when Kael was reincarnated, he would not remember his past lives. He would be born into the world, without any knowledge of who he truly was or the purpose that lay ahead of him. He would have to live many lives, each one building on the previous, until the moment came when he was ready to remember—and ready to find the Book of the Unknown.

The Loveday Method, a powerful tool for healing inherited trauma, was also part of this plan. It was not just a therapeutic practice—it was the mechanism through which Kael's soul would awaken to its purpose. The method was designed to help those who experienced the pain of their past lives to heal, to reconnect with the forgotten parts of themselves. But more importantly, it was through the Loveday Method that Kael's memories of the past would begin to resurface, and it would trigger the path to the Book of the Unknown.

As Kael was reborn, he would encounter many other texts—each one serving as a piece of the puzzle. The Akashic Library, the Book of a Thousand Lives, the Universe, the Book of Echoes, and The Lost Key were all part of the journey. These books were written to help humanity heal, to release inherited trauma and awaken the consciousness of those who were ready to understand the deeper truths of existence. They were all linked, part of a greater understanding of who we are and why we are here.

But even with all these texts, something profound was still missing. The Book of Echoes would be written, not just to heal the trauma of the past, but to guide humanity into the future. It would be the bridge between the past and the future—a future where healing was not a distant dream, but a reality. The future where the cure for every disease, both physical and mental, existed. Cancer, diabetes, heart disease—these afflictions would be cured. The healing would not just be for the body, but for the mind and spirit. The Book of Echoes would reveal how humanity could heal from the inside out, bringing about a new era of health and harmony.

But there was more yet to be discovered, hidden within the Book of Echoes and the Book of the Unknown. These texts were not just about healing—they were about understanding. Through the threads of time, humanity would come to understand who we really are, and why we are here. It was a journey not just of physical healing, but of spiritual awakening—a path that would lead to the full realisation of humanity's potential.

However, this understanding could not be rushed. The world was not ready yet. Humanity was still in the process of awakening, still struggling with the remnants of inherited trauma, still bound by the chains of fear and doubt. The Book of the Unknown, and the knowledge within it, could not be revealed until the time was right. The threads of time had to weave their way through the souls of humanity, bringing the world closer to the moment when it would finally be ready.

And so, the Book of the Unknown, hidden within the magical crystal, remained out of reach, waiting for the moment when humanity would unlock its secrets. The journey was not over; it had only just begun. Kael's soul, reincarnated again and again, would lead the way. The Loveday Method, the ancient books, and the hidden truths would all come together in time. But until then, humanity had to heal, to awaken, and to prepare for the day when the Book of the Unknown would be found, and the healing of the world would begin.

When will the time come? When humanity is ready. And when that moment arrives, the truth of who we are, and what we are capable of, will be revealed.

Chapter 5: The Stories You Are About to Read

Truth or Fiction? The choice is yours

The tales you are about to encounter are not just words on a page. Some may strike you as pure fiction, perhaps outlandish or too incredible to grasp, while others may resonate with an undeniable truth that feels like it's been woven into the fabric of your very being. But here's the crux: *I want you to decide.* You, the reader, are the final judge of what you believe.

In this collection, the lines between what's real and what's imagined are often blurred. Sometimes, reality is stranger than fiction, and what seems impossible at first may, in fact, hold the deepest truths. These stories come from different corners of existence: some are born of fantasy, while others are forged in the fires of lived experience. But the question I ask you to contemplate is this: What if the most extraordinary and unfathomable tales we dismiss as fantasy are, in fact, reflections of something we've yet to understand?

Every story, whether it seems improbable or grounded in reality, is a seed—planted in the hope that it will sprout a deeper awareness within you. You might read about someone's healing journey, a mystical vision, or a moment of revelation that defies all logic. You might shake your head in disbelief, or something deep within you might stir, recognising that these stories are a mirror of untold truths, ones hidden just beyond the veil of our everyday lives.

So, I ask you: will you open your heart to the possibility that these stories, regardless of their origins, carry a message that transcends mere words? Will you dare to believe that they might be more than just stories—perhaps glimpses of a world we cannot yet fully comprehend, waiting for us to acknowledge its existence?

The choice is yours. You may believe, or you may dismiss them as fanciful imagination. But here's what you need to understand: sometimes, the most unbelievable experiences are the ones that shift our perspective, that make us question everything we thought we knew about the world. The extraordinary often lives just beneath the surface of our everyday lives, and when we open ourselves to the possibility, we may find that what seemed impossible was simply waiting for us to see it in a different light.

So, as you turn the pages, as you dive into the mysteries that lie ahead, ask yourself: *What if?* What if these tales are not just stories, but clues to a deeper truth, waiting for you to unravel them?

Now, continue reading. The journey begins here. Will you believe what you read, or will you uncover something even greater than you imagined? The answer, as always, is up to you

Susanna and the Book of the Unknown: A Journey Into the Future

In the cold, bitter winter of 1463, Susanna lay in her cottage, burning with fever. The plague had gripped her body, its iron hold squeezing the life from her as she lay helpless, surrounded by the inevitable dark shadow of death. Her world had been small and fraught with suffering, as many others around her were also fighting for their lives. But, deep within her, Susanna had always felt there was something more—something beyond this dark time, something calling her, even in her moments of despair.

One evening, when the fever grew unbearable, something shifted. It wasn't just the sickness, it was something deeper—a calling, an overwhelming sense that she needed to leave her bed, to step into the cold and make her way into the forest. No logical explanation could have made her do it, but the pull was undeniable. She stumbled through the snow, the icy wind cutting through her, yet she couldn't stop. She walked as though some unseen force guided her forward, deeper into the woods, further from the village that held her death.

There, in the clearing, she saw it. A crystal. It glowed with an ethereal light, casting shadows in strange, shifting patterns on the snow-covered ground. The light seemed alive, almost as if it had a pulse of its own. Susanna's hand reached out instinctively, her fingers trembling as they touched the cool surface of the crystal.

The moment her skin met the crystal, everything changed.

Her vision blurred, her body felt weightless, and before she could understand what was happening, the world around her disappeared. The snow, the trees, the cold—all of it vanished as if it had never existed. Susanna felt herself being pulled, not through space, but through time itself. There was no sound, no sense of direction, just an overwhelming sensation of movement, as if the very fabric of reality itself was unraveling around her.

And then, she landed.

She opened her eyes to find herself standing in a place that was completely foreign to her. The air was unlike anything she had ever breathed—it was pure, clean, and full of life. The sky above her was a vibrant shade of blue, not clouded with the smoke of burning villages or tainted by the sickness that had ravaged her world. The land was lush, with fields of vibrant green stretching into the distance. The buildings she could see were magnificent yet simple, made from materials that shimmered with a light of their own.

It was a place that felt timeless, as though it existed far beyond the reach of anything Susanna had known.

Before she could comprehend what had happened, she noticed six beings approaching her. They were not human—no, they were something else entirely. They moved with a grace that was almost otherworldly, their forms radiant with light. There were no faces, no physical features to identify them. They were beings of pure energy, spiritual guardians, sent to guide her.

Without a word, the beings motioned for Susanna to follow, and she did, walking through this strange new world with a mix of awe and confusion. They led her down a wide path, past buildings that hummed with a gentle energy, towards a vast structure that seemed to pulse with life itself. It was a temple—ancient yet new, its stones shimmering with a soft, welcoming light.

Inside the temple, there was a single stone bed, surrounded by a warm, glowing aura. The beings gestured for Susanna to lie on it, and, without hesitation, she did. As soon as she lay down, a soft warmth enveloped her. It wasn't heat, but something far deeper—a healing energy that sank into her bones, soothing the aches of her body and calming the turmoil in her mind.

For the first time in what felt like forever, she was free. Her body was no longer sick. The fever that had burned her skin, the weakness that had crippled her, were gone. It was as if the plague had never touched her. Her mind, once clouded with fear and pain, was now clear, filled with a sense of peace that transcended anything she had known.

But the healing didn't stop there.

As the energy continued to flow through her, she felt something more. Memories, not her own, but glimpses of a future—a world far beyond her time. Visions of people living in harmony, their bodies and minds free from disease, their spirits alive with vitality. There were no more plagues, no more fear. People walked freely through vast cities, vibrant and full of life, their bodies whole, their hearts at peace. Susanna saw a future where mankind had unlocked the very essence of healing, where diseases of the mind, body, and spirit were no more

In the centre of the temple, a massive book appeared. Its pages were blank, but as Susanna approached, words began to form on them, as if the book itself was alive, responding to her presence. This was the Book of the Unknown.

The words within the book spoke of a future where all suffering had been erased, where mankind had reached its highest potential—physically, mentally, and spiritually. It was a future that seemed impossible in her time, yet Susanna knew, deep within her, that it was real. It was a future she had glimpsed, a reality that could be achieved, but not in her time. It was a truth that had to be hidden for the right moment—a truth waiting for the right people to understand it.

As the visions faded, and Susanna began to return to the place she had once known, she was filled with a profound sense of peace. She was healed—not just from the plague, but from every wound, every fear that had once plagued her soul. She had seen the future, and in it, she knew that healing was not a distant hope, but a certainty. The world she had witnessed would come to be, but it was not her time to reveal it. The knowledge had to be kept secret—for now.

The crystal that had brought her to this future world was still there, and as Susanna touched it once more, she was gently pulled back, this time with no fear, no pain. She awoke in the forest, where the cold night air hit her face, but this time, there was no sickness. She was no longer the woman who had stumbled through the snow, consumed by the plague. She was someone else entirely—someone healed, someone touched by the future that awaited humanity.

When she returned to her village, no one knew what had happened. To speak of what she had seen would have branded her a witch, a madwoman, and she could not risk that. So, she wrote it down—every detail, every image, every feeling. The Book of the Unknown, the crystal, the healing, the future—it was all captured in her manuscript, hidden away, a secret she could never share. But one day, she knew, someone would find it. And when they did, they would understand.

Until that day, Susanna lived quietly, her health restored, her mind and spirit free from the suffering she had once known. And in the depths of her heart, she held onto the truth of what she had seen: a world where healing was complete, where mankind would transcend suffering. She had touched the future, and it had healed her.

Was it a vision, or was it a glimpse of what is to come? The answer lies in the secrets of the past, waiting to be uncovered.

Could This Story Be More Than Just Legend? Was the Manuscript Ever Found? Read On, You Will Not Believe What Happens Next...

The story of Susanna, the young woman who was healed from the plague in 1463 and glimpsed the future of complete healing, has long been whispered about as just another village legend. A tale of mystical visions, strange crystals, and future worlds—stories that grow larger with each telling, a mystery of the past wrapped in the mystery of time. For centuries, the manuscript she wrote, detailing the Book of the Unknown, lay forgotten, buried beneath layers of history, seemingly lost forever. It was thought to be nothing more than a dream—too incredible to be real, too extraordinary to be true.

But what if this story is more than legend? What if the manuscript that Susanna left behind was not a fable, but a true account of her experience? Could the vision of a future free from suffering, a time of healing, be waiting to be unlocked? And if it were real, what happened to the manuscript? Could it have been found?

Many years passed. The village where Susanna lived slowly faded into history, its secrets buried in the earth and time. But fate, it seems, had other plans.

Chapter 6: The Manuscript

In the year 1923, a group of archaeologists, led by a determined historian named Dr. Emilia Graves, were excavating an old church on the outskirts of a small village in the English countryside. The church had been abandoned for centuries, but a series of mysterious old documents had surfaced, hinting at its forgotten past. Among the ruins, they unearthed a small, weathered chest—strangely intact despite the centuries that had passed. Inside the chest was an ancient manuscript, yellowed with age, but remarkably legible. The writing was in an old dialect, one that had long been forgotten. As Dr. Graves carefully opened the book, the first thing she saw was the title:

The Book of the Unknown.

Her heart raced. She had heard the legend of Susanna, the woman who had glimpsed the future, who had written of a time of healing, of a world free from disease. But this... this was more than a legend. This was real.

The manuscript was filled with Susanna's account: the vision of the crystal, her journey into the future, the beings of light who had healed her, and the Book of the Unknown that had shown her a world free of suffering. The words were filled with a clarity that left Dr. Graves stunned. The detailed descriptions of a future world were too vivid, too real, to be a mere fantasy.

Dr. Graves carefully transcribed the manuscript, working day and night to decipher the ancient text. As she read, she felt herself drawn deeper into Susanna's story. It was as if the book itself was alive, calling out to her, asking her to understand, to believe in the healing that Susanna had witnessed.

The more Dr. Graves read, the more she began to wonder: Was this the key to a future that humanity had forgotten? A future where healing is not just a possibility but a reality? Could the world Susanna saw truly exist, a place free from suffering?

But the true shock came when Dr. Graves reached the final pages of the manuscript.

In the last entry, Susanna's words took on a different tone, one of urgency, as if she had known that the time would come for this knowledge to be revealed. The final sentence read:

"This knowledge, though hidden for now, will one day be found. When the time is right, the world will be ready to heal. I have seen it. I have felt it. It is real. And when the day comes, they will know the truth. The healing that has been seen will be realised."

Dr. Graves felt a chill run down her spine. Could it be possible that the knowledge of this future world had been waiting, buried for centuries, until someone like her was ready to discover it? Could this manuscript, the Book of the Unknown, be the key to unlocking a time when the world would be free of disease, free of suffering? Was Susanna's vision not just a dream, but a reality waiting for humanity to claim?

As the manuscript continued to be studied, strange occurrences began to unfold. Those who read the book began to report feeling an overwhelming sense of peace, as if something deep within them had been healed. One by one, they spoke of an unshakable knowing that the world Susanna had seen was possible—that humanity could one day achieve what Susanna had witnessed: a world of healing, a world where illness and suffering were no more.

But then, something even stranger began to happen.

Dr. Graves, now deeply connected to the manuscript, began having vivid dreams—dreams of an angelic figure with no face, a being of light who guided her through strange, wondrous lands filled with life and vitality. She saw visions of a world free from disease, a place where the human spirit thrived, where peace and healing were natural, not an aspiration. It was the very world Susanna had written about.

In these dreams, the angelic figure spoke to her, not in words, but through deep, penetrating feelings, emotions that seemed to speak directly to her soul. The message was clear: The healing is not a far-off dream. It is waiting to be unlocked, and it begins with you.

Dr. Graves understood now. The manuscript was not just a piece of history—it was a living document, a key to the future. She had been chosen, just as Susanna had been, to carry this knowledge forward, to ensure that the world would one day awaken to the truth.

The manuscript had been found, but it was more than just a discovery. It was a call to action. A call to those who were ready to embrace a future where healing was possible. And the more people who read the manuscript, the more they felt that calling, that deep understanding that humanity was on the cusp of something extraordinary.

As the years passed, the knowledge contained in the Book of the Unknown began to spread. People all over the world read the manuscript and began to heal—not just physically, but mentally and spiritually. The vision of a world without suffering started to take root in the collective consciousness. It was a long road, but the first seeds had been planted.

The question remained—was this simply the power of belief, or was something far greater at work? Could the world that Susanna had glimpsed be on the horizon?

The manuscript, once thought to be a mere legend, was no longer a mystery. It was the beginning of a new world—one where healing was no longer a dream, but a reality.

And so, the journey continued. The Book of the Unknown had been found, and it was up to humanity to unlock its secrets. What happens next? That, dear reader, is the story yet to unfold.

Will the world awaken to the healing Susanna foresaw? Only time will tell, but one thing is certain—the key to that future has been uncovered. The question is, what will we do with it?

Was This the Book of the Unknown or Just a Manuscript of What is About to Happen?

The manuscript found by Dr. Emilia Graves was not just a collection of ancient words—it was the key to unlocking something much deeper, something beyond time itself. The question that haunted Dr. Graves as she deciphered the pages of Susanna's writings was: Was this the Book of the Unknown itself, or merely a fragment of it—a manuscript that foreshadowed what was yet to come?

While the manuscript clearly shared the same essence as the legendary Book of the Unknown, there was something different about it. The language, though ancient, felt strangely modern. The visions described in the text seemed to point not only to a world that Susanna had witnessed, but also to a world that was about to unfold. A future where humanity had transcended disease, where healing had become inherent in everyday life—was this just Susanna's vision, or was it the prophecy of a world yet to be realised?

As Dr. Graves continued to study the manuscript, she noticed something remarkable. The text spoke of events that had not yet occurred, a world where humanity would soon awaken to new possibilities—new forms of healing, new ways of thinking. It was not a history, nor a record of the past, but a promise of the future. The language hinted at something even more profound: that the true Book of the Unknown—the one that Susanna had glimpsed and been healed by—was still hidden, still waiting for the right moment to fully reveal itself.

The manuscript was, in a sense, a reflection of the original Book of the Unknown, yet it was also a mirror of what was to come. It described the world Susanna had seen, but in a way that suggested this vision was not fixed in time. It was something that could be realised—if humanity was ready. The manuscript, therefore, felt like a bridge between the past and the future, an invitation to those who were ready to understand the deeper truth about healing, both on a personal and collective scale.

Dr. Graves had been the one to find the manuscript, but now she understood it was her responsibility to help others find the key to what the book described. The world described in the manuscript wasn't something that simply existed in the future—it was waiting for humanity to step into it. But to do so, they needed to uncover the rest of the truth hidden within the original Book of the Unknown.

The question now was: Could the manuscript be the catalyst? Or was the true Book of the Unknown still out there, waiting for the moment when the world would be ready to embrace the truth about healing and transformation?

What Dr. Graves and the world were about to discover was far more than an ancient book. It was the beginning of a journey—one where the lines between past, present, and future would blur, and humanity would be faced with the ultimate question: Could the healing Susanna witnessed all those years ago finally come to pass?

The manuscript, though not the original Book of the Unknown, held within it a powerful truth: a future where disease, suffering, and pain could be healed—where humanity had the potential to create a world of peace and balance. And though the full book may still be hidden, its message had begun to take root.

As Dr. Graves pondered this question, she realised the manuscript was only the beginning. The healing that Susanna had glimpsed was within reach, but only if the world could unlock the rest of the truth. The key to that future had been placed in their hands. What would they do with it?

And so, the journey continued, the true Book of the Unknown still awaiting its full revelation. Was it waiting for Susanna's vision to unfold, or was the world now ready to make it a reality?

Chapter 7: Aelfric and the Book of the Unknown

A Journey to the Future

The year was 1066, and the winds of fate were shifting on the battlefield of Hastings. Aelfric, a simple soldier caught in the clash of kingdoms, had fought alongside the Saxons, feeling the heavy weight of both his sword and his grief. The battle had scarred him— not only with the injuries of war but with the images of death and destruction that haunted his every waking moment. The faces of those who had fallen, the cries of men and women torn apart by violence, were etched into his mind. His spirit, once strong and unwavering, had been shattered by the horrors he had witnessed.

As the years passed, the weight of his experiences grew unbearable. His heart was heavy with guilt, sorrow, and an unshakable feeling of loss. The memories of that day on the battlefield continued to haunt him, and he struggled to live a life free from the shadows of what he had seen.

One night, when the burden of his mind became too great to bear, Aelfric wandered into the forest. His legs moved without thought, driven by a sense of purpose he could not explain. There, beneath the cover of ancient trees, he found something that would change his life forever.

A crystal, nestled within the roots of a massive oak, gleamed softly in the moonlight. It wasn't a large crystal, but its glow was undeniable, drawing Aelfric towards it like a moth to a flame. He hesitated, unsure of why he was so compelled to touch it, but a force far stronger than his own will seemed to pull him forward.

When his fingers made contact with the crystal, a rush of energy flooded through his body, unlike anything he had ever felt. His vision blurred, his heart raced, and the ground beneath him seemed to dissolve. For a brief moment, Aelfric thought he was falling, spiralling into an abyss. His senses overloaded, and he could no longer tell where he was—where the forest had gone, or if the world he had known had completely disappeared.

And then, with a sudden and almost painful clarity, everything stopped.

Aelfric opened his eyes, and the world around him had changed. He was no longer in the forest, nor was he anywhere familiar. Instead, he found himself standing in a world that felt both alien and wondrous. The air was fresh, almost intoxicating in its purity. The sky was an endless expanse of blue, unlike any he had seen before, and the land stretched before him in vibrant greens and brilliant colours. The buildings were unlike anything he had ever encountered—sleek, shimmering, with tall towers and flowing structures that seemed to pulse with an energy of their own. There was a peacefulness in the air, an undercurrent of life that felt harmonious, untouched by war or suffering.

Before Aelfric could fully comprehend what was happening, a book appeared before him, seemingly out of thin air. It was large, bound in dark leather, its cover adorned with intricate symbols. Aelfric had never seen a book like this before. It seemed ancient yet alive, a silent presence that commanded his attention. The Book of the Unknown had arrived.

As he reached out to touch the book, it opened on its own, the pages turning, the words flowing like a river of knowledge. But as Aelfric began to read, he realised he was not simply reading the book. The words were not just written in the ancient tongue he knew—they were coming to life before his very eyes. The future unfolded in front of him like a vision, vibrant and detailed.

He saw a world without war, without disease. He saw people walking through cities filled with light, their bodies strong and free from illness. The technology and advancements he saw were beyond anything he could have imagined. Healing was not just a hope, but a way of life. People lived in harmony with the earth and with each other. He saw a future where suffering was a distant memory, where the human spirit had reached its highest potential.

But as Aelfric read, the visions grew even more powerful. The book revealed more than just the state of the world—it showed him the process of healing, the steps humanity would take to unlock this future. It showed him a time when physical ailments and mental struggles were no longer barriers. The human race had learned how to heal itself—not just in body, but in mind and spirit. It was a world that seemed almost beyond reach, but one that felt real, tangible, and possible.

Before Aelfric could absorb the full extent of what he had seen, the Book of the Unknown slowly began to close. As the final page turned, he felt a shift, as though something deep inside him was being awakened. The beings he had encountered—the six radiant, faceless figures—appeared once more, silently guiding him. A sense of peace flooded over him, the weight of his past lifting. The energy from the book had healed something within him, something that had been broken for so long.

One of the beings gently placed its hand on his shoulder, and without a word, Aelfric understood. The vision he had seen was not just a glimpse of a future—it was a call to action. It was a message for humanity, a message that would come in time, but one that needed to be shared. Aelfric's purpose was clear: he had been chosen to witness this future, to carry the knowledge of healing and peace back to his own world.

Suddenly, the world around him began to fade again, the figures, the book, and the future world vanishing into mist. Aelfric found himself back in the forest, standing before the crystal. The night was silent, the wind still. But the crystal was gone, and the air around him felt different—charged, as if something profound had shifted.

He walked back to his village, his heart no longer burdened by the memories of the battlefield. The visions of the future he had seen filled him with hope, not despair. His body, once aching with the weight of his experiences, now felt strong and renewed. The peace he had glimpsed in the future was inside him now. He carried it in his heart, knowing that this world of healing and harmony was not some distant dream—it was a future waiting to unfold, one that he had witnessed and was meant to share.

But even as he felt the peace in his soul, Aelfric knew he could not speak of what had happened. To do so would be to risk everything—to be branded as mad, or worse. The future he had seen was too far ahead, too different from the world he knew. So, he kept the secret locked deep within, carrying the message of healing and transformation, knowing that one day, when the time was right, the world would be ready.

Aelfric's life continued, but it was no longer defined by the battle he had fought, the loss he had endured, or the suffering that had consumed him. He had seen what was possible—a world of peace, of health, of unity. And although he could never share the full truth of what he had seen, he knew that the future he had glimpsed was within reach. All it would take was time. And that future, filled with healing, would one day come.

Was this just a vision, or was it a glimpse of what is to come? Only time will tell. But one thing is certain—Aelfric had seen the future, and it was a future of healing.

Chapter 8: Nicholas and the Book of the Unknown

A Journey of Loss and Healing

The year was 1939. Europe was drowning in darkness as the shadow of the Nazi regime swept across the land. The world, gripped by fear and hatred, would soon descend into a war that would tear nations apart. Among the millions caught in its vicious grip was a young boy named Nicholas. His family, Jewish and simple in their ways, lived in a small town where the streets once echoed with laughter. But that was before the soldiers came, before the world became unrecognisable, before hope became a distant memory.

Nicholas's world was shattered one fateful night when Nazi soldiers stormed into their home. The loud bang of the door breaking open echoed through the quiet house, the sound of boots clattering on the wooden floors. His parents, who had always shielded him from the horrors of the world, were now helpless. Nicholas could see the fear in their eyes, the helplessness that no words could dispel. The soldiers ordered them to pack their things—anything that would fit in a small bag. But it was all futile. They were marked for transport.

In a moment of panic and desperation, his mother bent down and whispered into his ear, her voice trembling with fear and love: "Run, Nicholas, run! You must survive. You must find the truth. Do not look back."

Without understanding fully what she meant, Nicholas did as his mother said. He ran. His small legs carried him as fast as he could, the sound of his own heartbeat pounding in his ears, drowning out the world. He glanced over his shoulder only once, his heart wrenching as he saw the soldiers dragging his parents away, their faces locked in fear, their lives torn apart in an instant. His mother's last cry echoed in his ears: *Run, Nicholas...*

But he couldn't stop. His mind was spinning. The only thing that mattered was escape, escape from the nightmare that was engulfing everything he loved.

As the days passed, Nicholas wandered through the streets alone, confused, hungry, and terrified. His world was dark, and his heart, once full of innocent joy, was now overwhelmed by sorrow and grief. He had lost everything—his home, his family, his future.

One cold night, feeling the unbearable weight of his sorrow and exhaustion, Nicholas stumbled through the forest near his town. It was there, in the moonlight, that he found the crystal.

At first, he thought it was just a strange rock or his mind playing tricks on him, but there was something unmistakable about it. The crystal pulsed with an otherworldly glow, beckoning him. It seemed to call out to him, whispering that it could take away his pain, his loss, that it held the key to something far greater than he could imagine. It was as though the crystal was offering him a way out of his suffering—a chance to leave behind the darkness that had swallowed his world.

Driven by a force he couldn't explain, Nicholas reached out and touched the crystal.

In that instant, everything changed.

The world around him blurred. His body was lifted from the earth, and he felt himself falling—not through space, but through time. He was being pulled into another realm, a place of pure light and peace. And then, as the dizzying feeling subsided, Nicholas found himself in a world unlike any he had ever seen.

The air was thick with life, rich and warm, unlike the cold, oppressive air of war-torn Europe. The landscape stretched out before him—vibrant green fields, golden skies, and towering structures that seemed to hum with an energy he couldn't comprehend. It was a world free from fear, free from suffering. It was a world where disease and death no longer reigned, where people lived in harmony with the earth and with each other.

Before him stood a grand temple, ancient yet radiant. The air inside was peaceful, heavy with an energy that soothed his weary soul. It was here, in this temple, that he encountered the beings of light—six radiant, faceless figures whose presence was both overwhelming and calming. They did not speak to him in words but communicated through feelings, emotions that surged through his very being.

They led him to the centre of the temple, where a pedestal stood, and upon it, the Book of the Unknown.

The book was unlike anything Nicholas had ever seen. Its cover shimmered with an inner light, and as he opened it, the pages revealed visions—visions of a future far beyond his time. He saw a world free from the plague of war, a world where all people were healed, both in mind and body. He saw cities full of light and people living in peace, without suffering, without the cruel grip of disease or death. It was a world of healing, a world where the very essence of life was full of light, harmony, and hope.

But as Nicholas read, the weight of his grief came crashing back. He saw his parents—his mother's face, pale and full of fear, his father, strong yet broken. The visions shifted, and he saw them being taken to the concentration camp, the place where their lives would end, where all that they had known would be destroyed.

His heart broke all over again. His pain, the loss, the fear—everything that had torn him apart in the real world was now filling him once more. But then, as if the beings of light could see the agony in his heart, they led him to a stone bed, bathed in a soft, healing light. They gestured for him to lie down.

As he did, a warmth enveloped him, not just in his body, but in his soul. The light that filled the room wasn't just physical—it was healing. It washed over him, taking away his sorrow, his guilt, his grief. The pain of losing his parents, the terror of that moment in his home, was lifted from his heart. He felt at peace, as though a burden had been removed. The visions of his parents' suffering softened, and he felt their love, their spirit, still alive in him, even though they were no longer with him.

The book was not just a vision of the future; it was a gift—a message that no pain, no loss, no war could ever truly destroy the spirit. His parents had suffered, yes, but they were not lost. They were part of the world of healing he had glimpsed. And he, too, was part of that world.

When the healing light faded, Nicholas stood up from the stone bed, his heart light, his spirit calm. He looked at the beings of light, who had guided him, and he knew that the world he had seen was not just a dream. It was a future that could be achieved—one day. And he, though young, could be part of making that future a reality.

As the crystal's glow slowly dimmed, he was returned to the forest, his body still reeling from the profound experience. He was no longer the boy who had fled his home in fear, lost and alone. He had seen the future. He had felt the healing that would one day come. His parents, though gone, were part of something greater. He would carry their love, their memory, with him always.

With renewed strength and purpose, Nicholas knew that the journey ahead was long. He had lost everything, but in the future, he had found the greatest gift of all: hope. The Book of the Unknown had given him the knowledge that healing was not a distant dream, but a real possibility—a truth waiting for humanity to claim.

Nicholas would never stop searching for the world he had seen, the world of peace and healing. Though the horrors of war had torn his life apart, he knew that one day, the world would be healed. And he would be there, part of it, carrying the message of hope that had been passed to him in the light of the crystal.

Could this be the end of the story, or the beginning of something greater? Could the future of healing, peace, and unity truly be within our grasp? Only time will tell, but Nicholas's journey was only just beginning.

Chapter 9: Zasa's Awakening

The Truth of Who He Really Was

The year was 1601, and the world was caught in the grip of uncertainty. In the vast stretches of Eastern Europe, amidst the upheaval of changing empires and the ever-present conflict between old traditions and new ideas, there lived a young man named Zasa. Though he lived in a small village at the edge of a great forest, Zasa's heart was far from the peaceful rhythms of rural life. He felt as though he had always been out of place—an outsider in his own world.

From a young age, Zasa had always sensed something was wrong.

His peers spoke of dreams of the future and the endless hopes of tomorrow, but Zasa's dreams were different. They were full of confusion and loss, fragments of places and faces he could not place. He often wondered why he was so deeply disconnected from the world around him. The townspeople saw him as strange, a dreamer with no clear purpose, and whispered behind his back, calling him a fool. But Zasa knew the truth. He didn't belong here.

There were nights when Zasa would sit alone by the fire, staring into the crackling embers, feeling the weight of something pressing on him, something he could not explain. He had no memory of a life before his birth, no knowledge of where he came from or why he felt so lost. He had tried to fit into his world—he had learned the ways of farming, the language of his people, the customs that had been passed down for generations. Yet none of it resonated with him. His heart longed for something beyond the boundaries of his village, beyond the life he had been born into.

One evening, as Zasa wandered the familiar forest that bordered the village, something happened. As the shadows of the trees stretched long and the last light of day faded into the night, Zasa stumbled upon a clearing he had never seen before. It was a strange place—an ancient stone circle, its stones weathered and worn, but still standing proud. The air was thick with an energy he could feel in his bones, a pull that drew him closer to the centre of the circle.

At the heart of the clearing, there was a small stone pedestal, upon which sat an object that radiated a soft, ethereal glow. Zasa's heart skipped a beat. It was a crystal—glowing with an inner light that seemed to call to him, like a whisper in his soul. Without thinking, he stepped forward and reached out to touch it. The moment his fingers brushed the surface, a wave of energy surged through him, a force so powerful it took his breath away.

Suddenly, the world around him began to shift. The trees, the ground, the very air seemed to blur and dissolve. Zasa felt as though he were being pulled into something far greater than himself. His body became weightless, his mind spinning with flashes of distant places—images of towering cities, landscapes that were both alien and familiar, faces that seemed to belong to lifetimes he had never lived. Time ceased to exist. There was only the overwhelming sensation of falling—of plunging into a deep, unknown realm.

When the spinning stopped, Zasa opened his eyes, and the world around him had changed.

He found himself standing in a vast, empty expanse. The sky above was dark, yet filled with the most vivid, beautiful stars he had ever seen. The ground beneath his feet was smooth, but it shimmered with a light that was not of this world. As Zasa looked around in awe, he felt a presence behind him—a being, standing tall and silent. It was not human, but it emanated an energy that filled him with warmth and peace.

The being spoke, not in words, but through feelings and images that flooded Zasa's mind. You have come to the place where the answers are waiting for you, Zasa. The truth of who you are has been hidden, but now it is time for you to see.

Zasa's heart raced. He had questions, so many questions, but no words could form in his mouth. The being, sensing his confusion, gestured for him to follow. Zasa did so, and they walked together, through a world of stars, where space and time seemed irrelevant. They walked past what seemed to be ancient portals, glowing faintly with an inner light. And then, they came to a door, carved from the very fabric of the universe, shining with an energy that spoke to Zasa's soul.

The being gestured for him to step forward. With trembling hands, Zasa reached out and touched the door. As he did, it opened, revealing a vast hall filled with glowing books—each one filled with the memories of souls across time. This was not a library of knowledge, but a library of existence, a collection of every life that had ever been lived.

The being led him to a single book that seemed to shimmer with a special light. As Zasa opened it, the pages revealed the truth of his existence. He was not merely the boy born in the village, lost and adrift in the world. He was a soul who had lived many lives, each one shaping the person he was now. His memories, his feelings of disconnection, were not the result of a broken world, but the echoes of countless lives he had lived across time. He had been a healer, a warrior, a teacher, a wanderer. Each life was a thread in the tapestry of his soul, each experience leading him closer to the truth of who he was meant to be.

But there was more. The being showed him a final truth—a vision of his purpose in this life. Zasa had been born into this world not by chance, but by design. His soul had chosen this life, knowing that it would be the one where he would finally awaken to the fullness of his being. He was not meant to live a life of quiet desperation or confusion. He had a higher purpose, one that would bring healing and wisdom to the world. He was a bridge between the past and the future, a soul chosen to unlock the potential of humanity.

The vision faded, and Zasa found himself back in the stone circle, the crystal still glowing softly in his hand. His heart swelled with a profound sense of peace. The questions, the confusion, the feeling of not belonging—they were all gone. He had seen who he truly was. He was a soul that had lived through countless lifetimes, and now, in this life, he was meant to share that wisdom with the world.

Zasa returned to his village, no longer feeling lost or out of place. His heart, now filled with the truth of his existence, knew exactly what he needed to do. He would no longer live a life defined by the expectations of others, or the confusion of his past. He had been chosen for a greater purpose—to awaken the world to the truth of who they really were, just as he had awakened to his own truth.

Though Zasa would face many challenges ahead, he was no longer afraid. He had found his place in the universe. He was not just a boy from a village—he was a soul with the wisdom of ages within him, and his journey had just begun.

The world will only know the truth when they are ready. And for Zasa, that time had come.

Chapter 10: Final Chapter

Or Is It Just the Beginning?

As Zasa stood at the edge of the ancient stone circle, the crystal now cool in his hand, a deep sense of understanding washed over him. The weight of his past lives, the echoes of countless souls, had all come together, revealing the truth of who he was—he was more than just a boy who had once felt lost in a world that seemed too vast, too cold, and too harsh. He was a soul on a path, a path that would not only lead him to discover his true self but also awaken others to their own potential.

The vision he had seen in the glowing halls, where the wisdom of all the past lives was stored, seemed as real as the world he now stood in. It had shown him his purpose: to heal, to teach, and to remind humanity that the answers they sought were already within them, just waiting to be awakened. No longer would he be the boy who felt disconnected, adrift in time. He now carried the wisdom of countless lives and knew that his soul's journey had led him to this moment.

But as the light of the crystal dimmed, Zasa felt something else stir within him—an awareness that this was not the end of his journey, but the beginning of something even greater. He had uncovered his true self, but what was next? What would happen now that he understood who he was? What was the next step?

The crystal, having served as the key to his awakening, had shown him the vastness of his soul's potential. But it had also revealed something more—a truth that humanity was not yet ready to see, a deeper understanding that was still hidden. There was more to discover.

Zasa had been shown the Book of the Unknown, a future where humanity was healed, a world where disease, suffering, and pain were no longer part of the human experience. He had seen the Book of Echoes, which carried the stories of countless souls, each leaving a mark on the collective consciousness. He had felt the wisdom of the Enchanted Spectacles, where the threads of time connected all beings in a deep, spiritual web.

But all of these were fragments of a larger truth—a truth that was not yet fully understood. Zasa's journey had opened the door, but there was more to explore, more to learn. And this was the part he could not yet fully grasp. He could feel it stirring inside him, a quiet, insistent whisper from the future. It was as though the universe itself was preparing him for something greater, something beyond his understanding. But it would not come all at once. The journey would take time, and the world would have to awaken in its own rhythm.

Zasa understood, deep in his soul, that the healing of the world—humanity's true awakening—would not happen overnight. It was a slow process, a gradual evolution of consciousness. But his role in this grand design was clear. He was not just a witness to the truth of the world. He was meant to be a guide, a teacher, someone who would help awaken others to the truth within themselves.

And so, with a deep breath, Zasa stepped forward, leaving the stone circle behind. The world around him was still dark, filled with pain, suffering, and uncertainty. But Zasa no longer saw the world through eyes clouded with confusion. He saw it through the eyes of someone who had glimpsed the future, someone who understood the healing that was possible. He knew that the light of this knowledge could not stay hidden forever.

He would begin small—perhaps with just one person, perhaps with many—but his journey had only just begun. The Book of the Unknown, the Book of Echoes, and the Enchanted Spectacles were just the first layers of the greater truth he had to share. The world would be healed, not through grand gestures or miracles, but through the quiet power of those who understood their true selves and shared that wisdom with others.

As Zasa moved through the world, he realized something else. The journey was not just about him. It was about everyone. Every person who walked the earth had the potential to awaken, to heal, and to reconnect with the truth of who they were. He was just the first step, but there were many more to come.

This was not the end of Zasa's journey—it was merely the beginning. He had found the truth of who he was, but now he had to live it. The future he had seen, the healing of the world, depended on every soul waking up to their own light, to their own power, and to the understanding that the world they sought was already within them.

The final chapter had yet to be written. The Book of the Unknown, the Book of Echoes, and the Enchanted Spectacles were just the beginning. The truth would unfold, not in a moment, but in a lifetime—Zasa's lifetime and the lifetimes of countless others who would awaken, one by one.

The journey of healing had begun, and it would continue for as long as it took, until the world was ready to see the truth. And in that truth, the future would be realised.

Was this the final chapter? Or was it only the beginning of something much greater? Only time, and the souls ready to awaken, would reveal the answer.

The Book of Echoes

The Legend of the Mystical Book:

Breaking the Cycle:

Whispers of an ancient legend speak of a book unlike any other—one not crafted with ink nor bound by mortal hands, but etched upon the very fabric of time itself. It is said that those who find it do not merely read its pages; they step into them, slipping through the veils of the past to walk paths long forgotten.

This is no ordinary chronicle of history. The book does not recount the deeds of kings or the rise and fall of empires. Instead, it reveals the hidden echoes of one's own soul—reliving the moments that shaped them before they even drew breath. It is a mirror, reflecting the silent wounds carried across lifetimes, unravelling the unseen threads that weave through one's pain, one's joys, and one's fate.

And yet, no temple has ever held it, no scholar has ever turned its pages. As the centuries passed, the greatest minds of every age came to question its very existence. Perhaps, they mused, it was never meant to be found in the physical world at all. Perhaps it was not a book, but a key—one that unlocks the boundless corridors of the mind, where time is not a river but an ocean, limitless and ever-reaching.

Still, the seekers remain. Not searching in dusty ruins or buried tombs, but within—the only place the book has ever truly existed. For those who dare to look, the past and present are but two halves of the same whole, and in their convergence lies the power to heal—not only oneself, but all of humanity.

And so, the search continues. Will you dare to open the book? Will you step beyond time and face the truths long hidden within its pages?

The journey awaits.

Chapter One: Whispers in the Dark

The wind carried the scent of rain as Elias stepped into the crumbling ruins of what had once been a temple. Moonlight slanted through the broken columns, bathing the ancient stone in silver. The silence here was thick, pressing against his ears like the hush before a storm.

He had spent years chasing a legend—a story so old, so buried in myth, that most had forgotten it ever existed. But Elias had not. For as long as he could remember, the whispers had haunted him, slipping into his dreams, speaking in voices that were not his own.

The book is not found. The book is remembered.

That was what the elders had told him when he first began his search. At the time, he had dismissed their words as riddles, the ramblings of those who had long since abandoned the quest. But now, standing here, he felt it—an undeniable pull, as though something just beyond the veil of reality was waiting. Watching.

He ran his fingers along the ancient carvings on the temple wall. They were smooth, worn by centuries of wind and rain, yet beneath his touch, they burned. Images flashed behind his eyes—shadows moving through time, flickering like candlelight. He staggered back, heart pounding.

This was no ordinary legend. This was a doorway.

Chapter Two: The Ink of Time

Elias awoke to darkness. Not the absence of light, but a deep, endless void, stretching beyond his sight. He was no longer in the temple. He was nowhere.

The voices returned, murmuring just beyond his comprehension. They swirled around him like a wind that carried no air.

"Who are you?"

The question was not spoken aloud, yet it echoed inside him.

"I—I don't know," Elias whispered.

A flicker of light appeared before him, swirling like ink dropped into water. It took shape—pages fluttering, letters shifting. A book, ancient and bound in leather that pulsed as though alive.

"Then read."

His hands trembled as he reached for it. The moment his fingers brushed the cover, the world shattered.

He fell.

Through time, through memory, through lifetimes not his own.

And the book—his book—began to write itself in the ink of his soul.

Chapter Three: The First Life

Elias hit the ground with a force that rattled his bones. He gasped, sucking in air that smelled of salt and fire. The world around him spun, shifting like the surface of water disturbed by a stone.

When the dizziness passed, he found himself standing on the edge of a vast desert. The sky overhead bled gold and crimson, the sun dipping toward the horizon. But this was no place he had ever seen before. The dunes stretched endlessly, and in the distance, black stone pyramids rose against the dying light.

He turned sharply at the sound of voices. A group of figures moved toward him, cloaked in flowing robes, their faces obscured by hoods. They spoke in a tongue Elias did not recognize, yet somehow, he understood.

"He has come."

"The echoes have awakened."

Elias stepped back, his pulse roaring in his ears. "Who are you?" he demanded, though his voice trembled.

One of the figures lowered their hood, revealing the face of a woman—ageless, yet worn by time. Her eyes were dark as the void he had fallen through, but filled with something deeper than knowledge.

"You are not here by accident, traveller," she said. "You are here because you have always been here."

The words sent a shiver through him. He looked down at his hands—only they were not his hands. The skin was darker, the fingers calloused from labour. He reached for his reflection in the shallow water pooled between the rocks.

The face that stared back was not his own.

Panic clenched his chest. "What is this?"

The woman stepped forward; her expression unreadable. "You are reliving what has been forgotten. The book does not show you what you wish to see. It shows you what you must remember."

Memories that were not his own rushed through his mind—flashes of laughter, the weight of a sword in his hand, the scent of burning incense in a temple long turned to dust. He knew this life. He had lived it.

"You must find the wound," the woman said. "Only then can you return."

Elias turned to her, desperate. "How do I wake up?"

She smiled, a sad, knowing smile. "You do not wake up. You remember. Only when you understand the pain of this life can you heal the one you left behind."

And then the world blurred again.

Chapter Four: The Wound beneath the Skin

Elias stood in a dimly lit chamber. Torches flickered against the stone walls, illuminating a figure kneeling before him. His heart pounded as he took an unconscious step forward.

He recognized this moment. It was a memory—a memory belonging to the man whose body he now inhabited.

The kneeling man was whispering words of mercy. His wrists were bound, his face bloodied. And in Elias's own hand, a dagger gleamed.

He knew what came next. He was the executioner.

A sharp pain tore through his chest, as if something ancient and broken was clawing its way to the surface.

This was the wound.

Not a scar on his skin, but on his soul. The choice he had made in this life—perhaps unwillingly, perhaps out of duty—had left an imprint so deep that even lifetimes later, it lingered.

The book had brought him here to face it.

Elias clenched his jaw, his breath ragged. He had no memory of who this man was, or why he had been sentenced to death. But it didn't matter. What mattered was the guilt—the weight he had carried across time, never knowing its source.

He lowered the dagger. The kneeling man locked up, eyes widening in shock.

"You choose a different path," the voice whispered.

A sudden force pulled Elias backward. The world cracked apart once more, and he felt himself spiralling, falling through darkness—until, at last, he hit the ground once more

Chapter Five: Awakening

Elias's eyes flew open. He was back.

The ruins surrounded him, silent and cold, just as he had left them. The ancient carvings beneath his fingers no longer burned. His heart pounded as he struggled to his feet, his breath uneven.

But something was different. The weight in his chest—the hollow, aching void he had carried his entire life—was gone.

He knew now.

The book was not an object to be found. It was a doorway, a mirror, a key to the past that had always lived within him. It did not simply reveal history—it revealed the scars of the soul, the unhealed wounds that shaped the present.

He had relived his first life.

And there would be others.

Elias turned, the wind stirring the dust at his feet. Somewhere beyond this place, beyond this moment, the book still called to him.

Because the past was not done with him yet. And neither was the journey.

Chapter Six: The Next Passage

Elias stood at the threshold of time, no longer questioning how or why the book had chosen him. The knowledge pulsed within him—this was not just his journey. He was merely the first. Others would come after him, seekers drawn by wounds they could not name, guided by the echoes of lives long past.

But he had to master it first.

The air around him shifted, the ruins blurring once more as the invisible hand of the book pulled him forward. His pulse quickened. This time, he did not resist.

As the world unravelled, Elias stepped willingly into the abyss.

Chapter Seven: The Physician's Hands

Elias landed hard, dust rising around him in a swirl. He blinked, adjusting to the dim candlelight of what appeared to be an old study. Shelves of aged manuscripts lined the walls, and the scent of herbs filled the air.

He caught his reflection in a polished brass mirror. His face was no longer his own—it was older, lined with wisdom and sorrow. His hands, strong and veined, bore the marks of someone who had spent a lifetime in healing.

He was a physician.

A knock at the door startled him. A woman entered, her face pale with worry.

"Master Loveday, he is fading fast. You must come at once."

The name sent a jolt through him. Loveday. The name felt familiar, yet foreign, as if it carried weight beyond this life.

He followed the woman down a stone corridor, his feet moving on instinct. Through another door, into a room where a man lay unconscious, his breaths shallow. The others in the room looked to Elias—no, to Loveday—with desperate hope.

Elias understood then. In this life, he had been a healer. A man devoted to understanding the wounds of the body, but more than that—one who had sought to heal wounds of the soul.

The book had brought him here for a reason.

He touched the dying man's hand. And in that moment, visions flooded his mind—flashes of trauma, grief, the burdens that had weakened this man beyond the physical. He saw the threads of pain that stretched across lifetimes.

This was it. This was the key.

Healing was not just about the present—it was about untangling the wounds of the past.

The Loveday Method was more than medicine. It was a bridge between time and self.

And now, Elias understood why he had been chosen.

Chapter Eight: The Others Who Follow

When Elias awoke again in the ruins, his body trembled, but his mind burned with clarity. The book had not just been showing him his past—it had been showing him a method, a path for others to follow.

He had healed something in himself. But now, he had the knowledge to help others do the same.

He was not the only one who needed this.

Word of the book would spread. Those who felt lost, those haunted by invisible pain, would seek him out. And when they came, he would guide them as the book had guided him.

The past was a wound. But it was also a cure.

And so, the Loveday Method was born—not just as a technique, but as a path through time, a way to reach into the echoes of the past and mend what had been broken.

The book was no longer just his burden. It was his gift. And soon, others would read its pages too.

Epilogue: The First Seeker

The first came at dusk, just as Elias knew they would. A woman, eyes dark with questions, stood at the edge of the ruins. She did not speak, but Elias could see it in her face—she carried the echoes too.

Without a word, he placed his hand over hers. The book whispered between them. And her journey began.

The Loveday Method and the Seekers of Time

Chapter Nine: The First Seeker's Descent

Elias watched the woman hesitate at the threshold of the ruins. The weight in her eyes was familiar—the look of someone burdened by something she could not name, haunted by a past she did not remember.

"You've felt it, haven't you?" Elias said, his voice calm but certain.

She nodded. "I don't know why I came here. Only that I had to."

Elias gestured for her to sit beside the flickering fire he had built in the centre of the ruins. He studied her for a moment. The book had not brought just anyone—it had chosen her.

"Tell me what you feel," he said.

She wrapped her arms around herself. "I don't know how to explain it. My whole life, I've had these... moments. Flashes of places I've never been. A fear of water, though I've never drowned. A pain in my chest, though no doctor can find anything wrong." She exhaled sharply. "It's like my soul remembers something my mind doesn't."

Elias nodded. "Then you're ready."

He reached out, placing his fingertips against her wrist. The moment he made contact, a pulse of energy rippled between them.

The book stirred.

She gasped, her eyes widening as the firelight dimmed, the world around them beginning to dissolve.

"Don't fight it," Elias murmured. "Let it show you."

The ruins faded, and the woman fell into the past.

Chapter Ten: A Life in the Water

The world was cold.

She opened her eyes to find herself on the deck of a wooden ship, the scent of salt thick in the air. The ocean roared beneath her feet, waves crashing violently against the hull.

She knew this place.

Though she had never seen it before, her body remembered. The weight of the ropes in her hands, the way the wind stung her cheeks—she had been here once.

"The storm is coming," a voice called behind her.

She turned to see a man—tall, broad-shouldered, with the look of someone who had spent a lifetime battling the sea.

And suddenly, she remembered.

He was her husband. And this was the night they were going to die.

The storm had come swiftly, swallowing their ship in its fury. She had drowned here, in these waters, the taste of salt burning her throat, her screams lost in the wind.

That was why, in this life, she feared the water. That was why the pain in her chest had never left.

Because she had never let go.

Chapter Eleven: The Release

Back in the ruins, Elias watched as she gasped, her body shaking, tears streaming down her face.

"It wasn't just a dream," she whispered. "It was real."

Elias nodded. "It was real once. But it does not have to be real now."

She clutched at her chest, breathing hard. "I never forgave myself. I tried to save him. I couldn't."

"You carried the guilt across lifetimes," Elias said gently. "But now you know. And now, you can release it."

She closed her eyes, inhaling deeply. And as she exhaled, the weight lifted.

The fear, the pain—it faded.

When she opened her eyes again, she was free.

The first healing was complete.

Chapter Twelve: The Others Who Come

Word spread. The first seeker became two, then five, then ten. Each came with an ache they could not explain—a fear, a sorrow, a wound deeper than flesh.

And one by one, Elias guided them.

A warrior who had lived a hundred battles, carrying guilt for the lives he had taken.

A woman who had always felt unseen, unaware that she had once been silenced by the hands of a tyrant.

A child who had been born screaming, afraid of the dark, not knowing that in another life, he had died alone in a prison cell.

Each journey through time unravelled the unseen wounds they carried.

Each healing rippled across lifetimes.

The Loveday Method was no longer just Elias's knowledge—it belonged to all who sought it.

Chapter Thirteen: The Guardian of the Book

Elias knew the book had chosen him for a reason.

He was not just its reader.

He was its guardian.

But something deeper called to him—something beyond himself, beyond even the seekers.

There was one final mystery the book had yet to reveal.

Who wrote it?

And why had it been left behind?

He could feel it now, whispering just beyond the edge of his understanding.

His journey was not over.

It was just beginning.

Origins of the Book & the Web of Journeys

Chapter Fourteen: The First Scribe

Elias had spent years guiding others through the Loveday Method, uncovering the wounds that stretched across lifetimes. Yet one mystery remained—the book itself.

It had appeared to him when he was ready; whispered its truths, and revealed the echoes of time. But where had it come from? Who had written it?

The answers lay within the book itself.

So, one night, beneath the silver glow of the moon, Elias placed his hands upon its cover and allowed it to take him back—not just into his own past, but to the first hands that ever held it.

The world fractured.

And when it reassembled, Elias found himself standing in the heart of an ancient temple, where a figure sat hunched over a stone slab, carving symbols into its surface.

The first scribe.

Chapter Fifteen: The Birth of the Book

The scribe was a woman, her robes threadbare, her fingers stained with ink. Elias knew, without being told, that she was the one who had first inscribed the book into existence.

And she was dying.

Her breaths were shallow, her body frail, yet she continued to carve, etching each letter with the weight of a thousand souls.

Elias stepped forward, though he knew she could not see him. He was only an observer here—a shadow in time.

"Why do you write?" he whispered, though no sound left his lips.

As if in answer, the woman murmured to herself, her voice weak but determined.

"Time is not a river. It is a circle. The wounds of one life become the echoes of another. This book must endure, so that those who come after me will remember."

Her chisel scraped against stone, and Elias saw the words forming beneath her hands.

"The soul does not forget. But the mind does. This book is the key to remembering."

A realization struck him like lightning; the book had never been written in ink. It had been written in time itself.

Each name, each passage, was a record of lives lost and found, wounds inflicted and healed.

This woman—this ancient scribe—had not created the book. She had merely been its first guardian, just as Elias was now.

And as she placed her trembling hands upon the stone tablet, a golden light pulsed from its surface, spreading outward in ripples through time.

The book had been born. Not as a physical object, but as a living force. It would appear whenever it was needed, to whoever was ready to see.

And now, Elias knew. He was not the first. And he would not be the last.

Chapter Sixteen: The Threads of Many Lives

Elias awoke with a sharp gasp, the ruins of the temple solidifying around him once more. His pulse pounded, but his mind was clear.

The book had existed for centuries. It had passed from one seeker to another, each of them unlocking its secrets in their own way.

And now, those who had been healed by the Loveday Method would soon discover—they, too, had a role to play.

The book did not belong to one person.

It belonged to all who sought to remember.

And across the world, across time, others were beginning to hear its call.

A young scholar in India, waking from dreams of a life she had never lived.

A warrior in the highlands of Scotland, feeling the echoes of battles fought before his birth.

A lost soul in the streets of New York, drawn to a bookshop where a certain ancient manuscript waited.

The journeys were many. The wounds were deep. But the book had always been there. Waiting. And Elias was ready to guide them.

Epilogue: The Next Guardian

One day, the book would leave him.

Elias understood this now. Just as the first scribe had passed it down through time, just as he had been chosen when the moment was right—soon, another would take his place.

But not yet. For now, the book was his to protect, his to share. He had begun as a seeker. Now, he was the guardian.

And the book... The book would live on.

Elias stood at the threshold of a new era, the weight of the Book of Echoes resting gently in his hands. He had always known this moment would come—the time when he would pass the sacred tome to its next guardian. The Book had chosen him, guided him, and now, it was ready to continue its journey through the annals of time.

As he gazed upon the ancient, leather-bound cover, memories of his own journey flooded back. He had begun as a seeker, yearning for knowledge and understanding. The Book had opened his eyes to the interconnectedness of all things, revealing the tapestry of existence woven through countless lives and experiences.

Now, as its guardian, Elias had fulfilled his role, guided others and safeguarding the wisdom contained within its pages. He understood that the Book was not his to keep; it was a living entity, meant to touch the lives of many, to inspire and enlighten across generations.

With a deep breath, Elias placed the Book upon a pedestal bathed in ethereal light. He whispered words of gratitude and farewell, knowing that its next guardian would soon arrive, drawn by the same call that had once beckoned him.

As he stepped back, the room seemed to shimmer, the air thick with anticipation. Elias smiled, a sense of peace washing over him. His journey with the Book had come to an end, but its legacy would endure.

The Book of Echoes would live on, continuing its sacred mission to illuminate the paths of those destined to seek its wisdom.

And Elias, now a part of its eternal story, would forever be connected to the endless chain of seekers and guardians, bound together by the timeless pursuit of knowledge and enlightenment.

In the quiet town of Ashcroft, nestled between rolling hills and ancient forests, lived Clara Bennett, a young historian with an insatiable curiosity for the past. Her days were spent amidst dusty manuscripts and forgotten relics, piecing together stories of those who had come before.

One crisp autumn morning, while exploring a long-abandoned estate on the outskirts of town, Clara discovered a hidden chamber behind a decaying bookshelf. Within, bathed in a shaft of golden sunlight, lay an ornate, leather-bound tome—the Book of Echoes. Its cover was adorned with intricate symbols that seemed to pulse with a life of their own.

As Clara reached out to touch the book, a warmth spread through her fingertips, and a cascade of visions flooded her mind. She saw glimpses of distant lands, ancient civilizations, and faces both familiar and foreign. Overwhelmed, she withdrew her hand, her heart racing with a mix of fear and exhilaration.

That night, sleep eluded Clara. The images she had seen haunted her thoughts, beckoning her to delve deeper. Unable to resist, she returned to the hidden chamber the next day, determined to uncover the secrets of the mysterious tome.

As days turned into weeks, Clara immersed herself in the Book's pages. Each chapter revealed stories of individuals from different eras, all connected by a common thread—their encounters with the Book of Echoes. She read of Elias, the first Guardian, who had dedicated his life to guiding seekers towards enlightenment. His journey resonated deeply with her, igniting a sense of purpose she had never felt before.

One evening, as Clara pored over a particularly enigmatic passage, the air around her seemed to shimmer. A soft, ethereal glow emanated from the Book, and before her stood a figure draped in robes of light.

Elias: "Greetings, Clara. You have been chosen."

Clara: "Chosen? For what?"

Elias: "To become the next Guardian of the Book of Echoes. Your journey has led you here, and now, the mantle passes to you."

Clara's mind raced. The weight of the responsibility pressed upon her, yet beneath it lay a profound sense of honour and destiny.

Clara: "But why me? I'm just a historian."

Elias: "It is precisely your love for history, your dedication to uncovering truths, which makes you worthy. The Book seeks those who can bridge the past and the present, guiding others towards understanding."

As Elias spoke, Clara felt a surge of clarity. The visions, the discoveries, all led to this moment.

Clara: "I accept. I will protect the Book and share its wisdom."

Elias smiled, a look of pride in his eyes.

Elias: "Remember, Clara, the Book is alive with the stories of countless souls. As its Guardian, you are now a part of this eternal tapestry. Trust in yourself, and in the journey ahead."

With that, Elias faded into the light, leaving Clara alone with the Book. But she no longer felt alone. The legacy of the Guardians before her, and the promise of those yet to come, filled her with unwavering resolve.

And so, in the quiet town of Ashcroft, a new chapter began. Clara Bennett, once a seeker of history, had become the Guardian of the Book of Echoes, entrusted with its timeless wisdom and the countless stories it held within.

As the new Guardian of the Book of Echoes, Clara Bennett embraced her role with a profound sense of purpose. She understood that the Book was not merely a repository of ancient wisdom but a living conduit, connecting souls across time and space. Her mission was clear: to guide seekers toward healing and enlightenment by helping them access the echoes of their ancestral pasts.

The Echoes of Sir Roland

The moment James turned the Book of Echoes to the next page, the words shimmered, shifting and twisting like whispers carried by the wind. A sudden pull, like an unseen force grasping his very soul, yanked him from reality. His breath hitched as the world around him melted into darkness, then flared into blinding light.

When his vision cleared, he was no longer in his living room.

The roar of battle consumed him. Swords clashed. Men screamed. Blood darkened the earth. The weight of heavy Armor pressed on his shoulders, a steel gauntlet encased his hand, gripping a sword that gleamed with fresh crimson.

"Sir Roland!" a soldier cried, panting as he stumbled toward James. "We've pushed them back. The village is ours!"

James blinked. Sir Roland? His mind reeled, but the instinctive knowledge was already there—he was Sir Roland. He knew the voice calling him, the weight of the sword in his grip, the taste of battle on his tongue. It was more than a dream; it was real.

A second knight approached, his armour glinting in the setting sun. Sir Cedric, James realized. A trusted comrade—but also a man of ruthless conviction.

"The commander's orders," Cedric said, voice hard. "Purge the village."

James stiffened. "What?"

Cedric's gaze did not waver. "They harboured our enemy. They must pay the price."

James turned toward the village. Smoke curled from thatched rooftops. Women clutched their children, wide-eyed with terror. A boy—no older than ten—stood frozen, his small hand gripping a wooden sword, a useless defence against the armed knights.

James's pulse pounded. *No. This isn't right.*

Cedric stepped closer; voice low. "We swore an oath, Roland."

James's throat tightened. He wasn't just a spectator in this memory—he could feel Sir Roland's turmoil, his duty warring against his conscience. Obedience meant safety. Defiance meant disgrace, exile... or death.

The boy locked eyes with him. Fear and desperation swirled within them.

James gritted his teeth. "No."

Cedric's brows furrowed. "What?"

James turned, raising his sword—not against the villagers, but against his own men.

"Stand down," he ordered. "These people are not our enemies."

Gasps rippled through the soldiers. Cedric's eyes darkened. "You would defy the commander?"

"I would defy butchery."

The silence stretched like the pull of a bowstring before release. Then Cedric sneered, stepping back. "Then you are no knight of this order."

James's fate was sealed at that moment. He knew it, felt it in his very bones. The condemnation, the loss of everything he had built—his knighthood, his honour—was now dust in the wind.

But the boy still breathed. The villagers still lived.

And that was enough.

Echoes in the Present

James gasped as reality came rushing back. His fingers clawed at his chest, searching for armour that was no longer there. The weight of the sword was gone, replaced by the cold, familiar silence of his apartment.

But the guilt remained.

He pressed a hand to his forehead, his breath unsteady. He had been Sir Roland. He had felt the crushing weight of his decision, the sting of exile. But more than that—he had felt his atonement.

A knock at the door startled him. Clara's voice followed. "James? You, okay?"

He hesitated, then exhaled slowly. "Yeah... Come in."

She stepped inside, concern etching her features. "You looked like you were in a fight for your life."

James chuckled dryly. "In a way, I was."

She sat across from him, waiting. She always waited, never pushed. That was why he trusted her.

So, for the first time in years, James spoke. Not in half-truths. Not in deflections. He told her everything—about Sir Roland, about the battle, about the choice he had made and the exile that followed.

When he finished, Clara was silent for a long moment. Then she said, "He sounds a lot like you."

James's breath hitched. "What do you mean?"

"You both did what was right, even when it cost you everything." She leaned forward. "You've spent years punishing yourself for choices you made in war, James. But what if your purpose—your redemption—comes from helping others find their own?"

The words struck deep. He had saved those villagers as Sir Roland... but he was still saving people now, wasn't he? Every time he reached out to a fellow veteran, every time he offered an ear, every time he helped someone else find their footing.

The past wasn't a weight meant to drag him down.

It was a guide, leading him forward.

A New Purpose

In the weeks that followed, James felt the shift within him. He spoke at group meetings, shared his story with others who had walked the same path of guilt and self-doubt. He no longer carried the burden alone.

His family noticed the change—the light returning to his eyes, the way he no longer flinched away from their concern. He laughed more. He lived more.

One day, as he placed the Book of Echoes back on the shelf, he ran his fingers along the worn cover. He wasn't sure how it worked, why it had shown him that past life.

But he was grateful.

Because some echoes were not meant to haunt. Some were meant to heal.

And James had finally heard them.

Echoes of Healing

Clara found Elena sitting on the park bench, her gaze fixed on nothing in particular. The woman's face was pale, worn from too many sleepless nights, her fingers twisting the fabric of her coat in restless movements.

Clara approached cautiously. "Elena?"

Elena blinked, as if waking from a dream. "Oh. Clara." Her voice was hoarse, like she hadn't spoken much in days. Maybe weeks.

Clara sat beside her, silent for a moment. The air was thick with unsaid things. Finally, she said, "I know the weight you're carrying."

Elena gave a bitter laugh, shaking her head. "No. You don't."

Clara reached into her bag and pulled out the Book of Echoes. She had been unsure at first, hesitant to share its power with others. But now... now, she knew that Elena needed to see.

"Elena," she said softly, placing the book between them. "Let me show you something."

Elena frowned but hesitated only for a moment before reaching out. As soon as her fingers touched the ancient cover, the world shifted.

The Healer's Burden

Elena found herself in a dimly lit cottage, the scent of herbs and burning incense thick in the air. A fire crackled in the hearth, casting flickering shadows across the walls lined with vials, dried plants, and handwritten scrolls.

But it was the woman at the centre of the room who caught Elena's breath.

The healer.

She knelt beside a still form, a young girl, her small hand cold in the healer's grasp.

"She was the last of them," a voice whispered.

Elena turned. An old man stood in the doorway; his face lined with sorrow. "The plague has taken them all."

The healer's hands trembled. "I tried," she whispered. "I did everything I could."

Elena could feel it—the weight of helplessness, the soul-crushing despair. The healer had fought, had spent nights grinding herbs, boiling roots, praying to any gods who would listen. But in the end, it had not been enough.

She let out a shuddering breath. "What is the point of my work if I cannot save them?"

The old man stepped closer, resting a hand on her shoulder. "Because there will always be more who need you."

The words settled in the air, lingering.

The healer swallowed. The grief was still there, it would always be there, but it did not have to be a tomb.

Slowly, she stood, wiped her tears, and turned toward the rows of herbs and remedies that lined her walls.

Not for the ones she had lost. But for those she could still save.

A Path Forward

Elena gasped, her body jolting as she was pulled back into the present. She clutched the edges of the bench, her breath uneven, her heart pounding.

Clara waited.

Elena pressed a hand to her chest. "I… I felt it. Her pain. It was like… it was mine."

Clara nodded. "Because it was."

Elena's vision blurred with unshed tears. "She lost them. All of them. And yet… she kept going."

"She found a way to honour them," Clara said gently. "Not by forgetting, not by replacing them, but by using what she had to help others."

Elena swallowed, her fingers curling into fists. "I don't know how."

"You don't have to know yet," Clara assured her. "But maybe... maybe there's a way to take what you've lived through and make something out of it."

Elena closed her eyes. For the first time in months, there was no void.

There was something else.

A possibility. A path.

She turned to Clara, her voice barely a whisper. "Where do I start?"

Clara smiled, reaching for her hand.

"We'll figure it out together."

Echoes That Heal

Days turned into weeks, and Elena's steps were slow at first. Small. She began volunteering at grief support groups, simply listening, being present. Then she started organizing small acts of kindness—sending letters to bereaved parents, donating to children's charities.

Her grief was still there, a companion she would never part with.

But it no longer chained her.

One day, as she placed a single white flower on her child's memorial, she whispered, "I will carry you forward."

And somehow, she knew, deep in her heart—her child's love would echo on in every life she touched.

The Third Seeker: A Leader's Doubt

Marcus sat in Clara's small office, his hands clasped together, fingers drumming restlessly. His broad shoulders, which usually carried the weight of others with ease, now sagged under an invisible burden.

"I don't know if I can do this anymore," he admitted. His voice was steady, but the weariness in his eyes betrayed him.

Clara tilted her head. "What makes you say that?"

He let out a humourless chuckle. "Because I'm failing. I can feel it. Every decision I make feels like a gamble, and I can't shake the fear that one wrong step will bring everything crashing down."

She studied him for a moment, then reached for the Book of Echoes. "Maybe it's not failure you fear," she said gently. "Maybe it's the weight of responsibility."

Marcus frowned as she slid the book toward him. "What is this?"

Clara smiled knowingly. "A perspective you might need."

Hesitantly, Marcus placed his hands on the book. The moment his fingers met the cover, the world blurred.

The Chief's Trial

Marcus blinked and found himself somewhere else.

The scent of rain-soaked earth filled his lungs. The dense jungle around him buzzed with life—chirping insects, distant calls of unseen creatures. A fire burned at the centre of a gathering, casting flickering shadows on a circle of warriors.

He looked down. Fur-lined garments. Hands calloused by labour. A ceremonial pendant carved from bone rested against his chest.

He was the chief.

A voice broke through the murmurs of the gathered warriors.

"The drought has taken the crops. The hunters return empty-handed. The people are afraid."

Marcus turned toward the speaker, an elder with piercing eyes. He felt the weight of those eyes pressing against his soul.

"What will you do, Chief?" another warrior asked.

The question sent a chill through Marcus's spine.

He didn't have an answer. His people waited. Expectant. Trusting.

And yet he doubted.

Would his decision lead them to survival, or to ruin? What if he chose wrong?

His fingers curled into fists. He could not show weakness.

But then...

A voice whispered in his mind, echoing from the depths of the Book.

Doubt is not a weakness. The realization struck him as if the earth itself had shifted beneath his feet.

Slowly, he exhaled, straightened his shoulders, and spoke.

"We do not know what tomorrow will bring," he admitted. "But what we do know is that we are strong. We have faced worse, and we endure. We do not lead with fear. We lead with faith—in ourselves, in each other."

Silence stretched for a moment. Then, a warrior nodded. Another gripped his spear tighter, hope rekindled in his eyes.

Marcus felt something stir within him.

Leadership was not about having all the answers. It was about standing firm, even when the path was unclear.

And that was enough.

Returning With Clarity

With a sharp inhale, Marcus was back.

The firelight faded, replaced by the soft glow of Clara's lamp. His heart still pounded as if he had truly stood before his people in the jungle, as if the weight of their expectations had been his own.

And maybe... it had been.

Clara studied his face. "What did you see?"

Marcus exhaled, rubbing a hand over his face. "A leader. A chief. He had no answers, but he led anyway." He looked up, his voice steadier. "He was afraid, just like me."

Clara nodded. "Because doubt is part of leadership."

Marcus let the thought settle. "I've spent so much time thinking I needed to be certain about everything. That if I had doubts, it meant I wasn't fit to lead."

She smiled. "And now?"

He sat up straighter, something new—or perhaps something rediscovered—in his eyes.

"Now I understand. Leadership isn't about never questioning yourself. It's about moving forward despite the questions."

He stood, feeling lighter. The burden was still there, but it no longer felt impossible.

Before he left, he turned to Clara. "Thank you."

She simply nodded. "Lead well, Marcus."

And he would.

This time, without fear.

The Fourth Seeker: An Artist's Block

Sophie sat in her dimly lit studio, staring at the blank canvas before her. The brushes, once extensions of her soul, now felt foreign in her hands. The colours in her paints had lost their vibrancy.

She let out a sigh, rubbing her temples. Nothing. No inspiration, no passion—just an empty void where her creativity had once thrived.

Clara watched her for a moment before setting the Book of Echoes on the table between them.

Sophie glanced at it warily. "What is this?"

Clara smiled. "A mirror. A doorway. A reminder."

Sophie hesitated, but something in Clara's tone—gentle yet certain—made her reach forward.

The moment her fingertips touched the cover, the world shifted.

The Artisan's Rebellion

Sophie found herself in a small, dimly lit workshop, the scent of clay and burning wood filling the air. A woman sat at a worktable; her hands stained with pigment as she carefully carved intricate symbols into a ceramic vase.

Sophie could feel the artisan's heartbeat—steady, yet defiant.

The door creaked open. A man in foreign armour entered, his gaze sweeping the room with suspicion. Sophie felt the artisan still, her chisel pausing mid-stroke.

"Show me your work," the man demanded.

The artisan wiped her hands and lifted a seemingly ordinary plate, its designs simple, traditional. The soldier glanced at it, grunted in approval, and left without another word.

But the moment the door shut, the artisan let out a breath—and turned over the true piece she had been working on.

Hidden beneath the surface were forbidden symbols—messages of resilience, resistance, hope.

Sophie's breath caught. The artisan had not been creating for beauty alone. She had been fighting—in silence, through art, through the defiance of creation itself.

Even when the world tried to erase her culture, she carved it back into existence.

The realization crashed over Sophie like a wave.

Art was not just expression. It was survival.

The Canvas Speaks Again

With a sharp gasp, Sophie returned.

The dim studio came into focus. Her breath was unsteady, her hands trembling—not with fear, but with understanding.

Clara watched her carefully. "What did you see?"

Sophie swallowed; her throat dry. "She created because she had to. Because if she didn't, her people's stories would be erased."

Clara nodded. "And what does that mean for you?"

Sophie turned to her empty canvas. It was no longer empty. She could already see the strokes, the colours, the unspoken words waiting to be painted.

Her voice was quiet, but sure. "That I've been looking for inspiration in the wrong place."

She picked up a brush, dipped it into the paint, and began.

Not to impress. Not too perfect.

But to speak.

Echoes of Transformation

As Clara guided each seeker through the Book of Echoes, she saw the profound transformations unfold before her eyes.

Marcus, once paralyzed by doubt, now led with both strength and humility.

Elena, consumed by grief, found purpose in honouring her child through compassion.

Sophie, lost in artistic silence, rediscovered her voice through the power of creation.

Each of them had stepped into the past, not to escape their struggles, but to understand them—to carry forward the lessons of those who came before.

Clara closed the book gently, a quiet reverence in her heart.

Because in the echoes of history lay not just the past, but the keys to healing, purpose, and evolution.

The Book of Echoes Finds Another Way

Chapter Seventeen: The Forgotten Name

London, 1893.

The gas lamps flickered in the thick London fog as Margaret Lovell tightened her coat against the chill. The city streets were alive with whispers—cobbled alleys echoing with the clatter of carriage wheels, the murmur of merchants, the faint chime of church bells lost in the smog.

But Margaret heard something else.

Something older.

Something calling.

She had felt it for weeks—a strange pull, an invisible thread winding through the fabric of her mind. It had started with dreams.

Visions of a book.

A book she had never seen, yet somehow remembered.

She had spent every night searching—through archives, through forgotten texts in the dim-lit corners of the British Museum's library. But no matter how many pages she turned, she never found it.

Because it did not exist on any shelf.

Not yet.

Chapter Eighteen: The Bookshop on Fleet Street

It was on a Tuesday that Margaret found the book.

Or rather, that it found her.

She had been wandering aimlessly, lost in thought, when she saw the flickering candlelight inside a narrow bookshop tucked between two larger buildings. The kind of shop that shouldn't have been there—the kind no one remembered until they needed it.

She pushed open the heavy wooden door, and a small bell chimed overhead. The scent of old parchment and ink filled her lungs, familiar yet foreign.

Behind the counter, an old man with silver-rimmed spectacles looked up. His gaze was knowing, as if he had been expecting her.

Margaret hesitated. "I—" She stopped, uncertain of why she was even here.

The man simply nodded and turned away, disappearing into the maze of towering bookshelves.

Margaret followed.

Through narrow corridors of forgotten knowledge, past dust-covered books filled with languages she couldn't read. Until, at last, he stopped before a lone wooden pedestal.

And there, resting on its surface, was the book.

A leather-bound book, its cover unmarked, as though its title had long since faded from time itself.

Margaret reached out, her fingers barely brushing its surface. The world cracked apart.

Chapter Nineteen: A Life Once Lived

She was falling.

Through time. Through memory. Through herself.

The fog of London disappeared, replaced by the scent of salt and damp earth. The flickering gas lamps faded into torchlight.

She was no longer in 1893.

She was someone else.

She opened her eyes and found herself standing on the edge of a towering cliffside, waves crashing violently below.

Her hands were bloodstained.

And behind her, a voice called out—a voice filled with grief, anger, betrayal.

"Margaret!"

She turned. And she remembered everything.

Chapter Twenty: The Buried Past

It happened centuries ago.

A different name. A different life.

She had lived and died on this very cliff.

She had been the daughter of a noble house, accused of treason against the crown. But the truth had been buried—only she had known what really happened.

And someone had made sure she never spoke of it again.

Someone had pushed her.

Sent her tumbling into the ocean, her last breath stolen by the waves.

And now, she was here again.

The book had not brought her back to relive the moment.

It had brought her back to understand it.

She had not been weak. She had not been a victim.

She had been silenced.

And for lifetimes, that silence had followed her.

It was why, even in 1893, she had always felt unseen.

Why she had never truly found her voice.

Until now.

Chapter Twenty-One: The Guardian's Choice

Margaret woke with a gasp.

She was back in the bookshop.

The old man watched her, his face unreadable.

"The book does not show us what we wish to see," he said at last. "Only what we must."

Margaret's hands trembled, the memory of the cliffside still fresh, as though the salt water clung to her skin.

"I—" she swallowed. "I was murdered."

The old man nodded. "And now, you remember."

She looked down at the book, still resting before her.

She had spent lifetimes running from the truth. But now she understood.

The book did not just reveal the past.

It healed it.

And with that knowledge, a new understanding settled over her.

This was not just her journey.

She was not the only one who had forgotten.

And if she could remember, she could help others do the same.

Margaret closed the book.

And when she looked up, the old man was gone.

The bookshop was empty.

And in her hands, the book had become hers.

She was no longer just a seeker.

She was the next guardian.

And the journey had only just begun.

Epilogue: The Threads of Time

Elsewhere, in another time, in another place…

A new seeker was awakening. The book had begun calling to someone else. And the cycle would begin again.

Because time is not a river, it is a circle. And some echoes never fade.

A New Seeker; A Different Time

Chapter Twenty-Two: The Astronaut and the Book

Year: 2147
Location: Lunar Colony, Mare Serenitatis

The stars stretched endlessly above Dr. Kieran Voss; a silent ocean of darkness interrupted only by the glowing Earth far in the distance. He stood at the observation deck of Lunar Base ECHO-7, the glass panel before him revealing the barren beauty of the Moon's surface.

For months, he had been having dreams.

Visions of places he had never been. Voices speaking in languages he did not know, yet understood. A name— one that did not belong to him, yet felt like his own.

And most of all, a book.

A book that did not exist in any archive, any database, or any historical record.

Until today.

Because it had appeared.

Not on Earth. Not in a museum.

But here, on the Moon.

Chapter Twenty-Three: The Artifact

It had been a routine excavation. The research team had been scanning an ancient lunar crater, searching for signs of deep-space matter when the scanners picked up something impossible.

A structure.

Buried beneath the Moon's surface.

A door that had no right to exist.

Kieran had led the investigation, unsure if what they had found was human-made or something... else. But when the excavation revealed the book, everything changed.

No oxygen. No life. No reason why it should be here, perfectly preserved in an airless vacuum.

Yet there it was.

Bound in leather that looked untouched by time, its pages filled with words that shifted and changed when he tried to read them.

And the moment he touched it—

He fell through time.

Chapter Twenty-Four: The Fall Through Memory

The sterile walls of the lunar base vanished.

The hum of machinery, the weightlessness of low gravity—gone.

Kieran's body plummeted through space, through light and darkness, through the unseen corridors of time itself.

Until his feet hit the ground.

And he opened his eyes to a battlefield.

Chapter Twenty-Five: The Soldier He Once Was

The air was thick with smoke. The sky burned red.

Kieran stood in the middle of a war he did not recognize, but somehow knew intimately.

The weight of armour pressed against his body. A sword—not a laser tool, not a mechanical instrument, but a crude, bloodstained blade—was clutched in his hand.

And around him, men screamed.

The clash of metal. The scent of death.

This was Earth, but not the Earth he had known.

This was the 10th century.

And he had been a warrior.

Flashes of memory hit him like an explosion—

A kingdom at war. A battle fought for a cause long forgotten.

And a betrayal that had cost him his life.

"You were the commander," a voice whispered, echoing through the battlefield.

Kieran turned.

A soldier stood before him, helmet cracked, blood running down his face. His eyes burned with rage and sorrow.

"You led us here. You led us to die."

The guilt hit Kieran like a knife to the chest.

Because he remembered.

He had ordered the charge. He had believed in victory.

And instead, they had all perished.

He had perished.

And now, over a thousand years later, the book had brought him back.

To face it. To understand. To heal.

Chapter Twenty-Six: The Choice That Was Never Made

The battle raged around him, but Kieran no longer felt like just a soldier.

He was both the past and the present, trapped between who he had been and who he had become.

And suddenly, he saw it—

A single moment in time. The moment before the charge. The moment before he doomed them all.

"What if you had chosen differently?" the voice whispered again.

For centuries, for lifetimes, he had carried the guilt of this war.

But now, he was being given the chance to change it.

Kieran inhaled sharply.

Then, for the first time in a thousand years, he spoke the words he had never spoken:

"Hold the line. Do not charge."

And the world shattered.

Chapter Twenty-Seven: The Awakening

Kieran's eyes snapped open. He was back.

Back in the lunar base, back beneath the artificial lights, the oxygen thrusters humming softly in the walls.

The book rested in his hands.

Only now, the cover had changed.

No longer blank, it bore a single inscription.

His name.

Kieran exhaled, his body shaking. He had been so sure the visions were just fragments of his imagination. But now, he knew the truth.

The book did not belong to the past.

It existed outside of time, waiting for those who needed it, revealing the wounds buried deep in the fabric of the soul.

And he was not the first to find it.

Others had held it before him.

Others would hold it after him.

But for now, in this moment, in the year 2147, on the surface of a dead moon,

It was his.

Epilogue: The Next Guardian

Kieran sat alone in the observation deck, staring at the Earth as it hung in the void.

The book lay open before him, its pages blank.

Waiting.

He was not just an astronaut anymore.

He was not just a scientist.

He was a seeker.

And soon, just as it had called to him, it would call to another.

Because time is not linear.

It is a circle.

And some stories are never truly finished.

Only waiting to be remembered.

Another Seeker, Another Time

Chapter Twenty-Eight: The Samurai and the Book

Kyoto, Japan — Year 1602

The cherry blossoms were in full bloom as Hana Ishikawa knelt beside the koi pond in her family's garden. The wind carried the scent of spring, rustling through the silk of her kimono.

Yet despite the beauty surrounding her, she could not shake the unease curling in her chest.

For weeks, she had been plagued by visions—strange and impossible memories of battles she had never fought, of swords clashing in the dead of night, of blood staining her hands.

But the strangest of all was the book.

A book she had never seen, yet felt as though it had always been with her.

And today, it arrived.

Wrapped in fine silk, an unmarked leather-bound book had been left outside her chamber door with no explanation, no sender.

Only a single note tucked within its pages:

"It is time to remember."

Her hands trembled as she turned the first page.

And in an instant, her world shattered.

Chapter Twenty-Nine: The Warrior She Once Was

Hana fell.

Through darkness. Through memory.

Through time.

When she opened her eyes, she was no longer in Kyoto.

She was standing in the middle of a battlefield.

Her body was different—stronger, armoured, poised for battle. The weight of a katana pressed into her palm. The sound of war drums pounded in her ears.

She was no longer Hana Ishikawa, daughter of a noble house.

She was Takeo, a samurai warrior, and this was the night he would die.

Chapter Thirty: The Last Stand

Hana's mind screamed in confusion, but her body remembered.

She knew how to move, how to fight.

Knew the men standing beside her, warriors sworn to the same cause, their faces twisted in grim determination

This was the Siege of Osaka.

And she—he—had fought for the wrong side.

The enemy forces outnumbered them five to one. The battle was already lost.

But they had fought anyway.

Because that was the samurai way.

Because Takeo had sworn to die with honour.

But as Hana stood there, trapped in his body, watching the enemy descend like a black wave, a single thought pierced through the chaos:

"What if I had lived?"

She had always accepted this fate in the past.

But now, centuries later, the book had brought her back for a reason.

To change the story.

Chapter Thirty-One: Breaking the Cycle

The enemy charged.

Takeo's men braced for death.

But Hana did something different.

She dropped her sword.

The warriors beside her gasped. The enemy hesitated.

And at that moment, she spoke.

"Enough," she said.

And for the first time in any lifetime, Takeo did not fight to die.

He fought to survive.

Chapter Thirty-Two: The Return

Hana gasped as she was pulled back.

The battlefield vanished. The past faded into the wind.

She was kneeling once again beside the koi pond, the book resting in her lap.

Only now, she understood.

She had spent lifetimes believing that honour meant dying for a cause.

But today, she broke the cycle.

Honor was not in death.

It was in choosing to live.

And now, she was free

Chapter Thirty-Three: The Path of the Book

The book was still open.

But its pages were blank.

Waiting.

She had rewritten her past. And now, like those before her, she knew the truth—

This book was not just hers.

It was a gateway.

A path through time, meant for those ready to face the echoes of their past.

And somewhere, in another time, in another place—

It was calling to someone new.

A New Seeker in the Industrial Age

Chapter Thirty-Four: The Engineer and the Book

Manchester, England — Year 1851

The air was thick with the soot of progress as Thomas Whitaker navigated the bustling streets of Manchester. Steam-powered machines clattered in factories, and the hum of innovation was palpable. As a skilled engineer, Thomas was at the heart of this transformation, contributing to the marvels of the Industrial Revolution.

Yet, amidst the triumphs of engineering, he felt an inexplicable void—a sense that something essential was missing. Lately, his nights were restless, haunted by vivid dreams of a mysterious book and a life he couldn't recall.

One evening, as he returned home, a peculiar package awaited him. Wrapped in aged parchment, it bore no sender's mark. Inside, he found an unmarked leather-bound book. His heart raced; this was the book from his dreams.

With trembling hands, Thomas opened it, and the world around him began to blur.

Chapter Thirty-Five: The Weaver's Tale

Thomas found himself in a dimly lit cottage, the rhythmic clanking of a loom filling the space. He looked down to see calloused hands deftly weaving threads—a stark contrast to his usual ink-stained fingers.

He was no longer an engineer but a weaver in the early 18th century. The realization hit him hard; this was a past life.

Memories flooded back: the struggle to make ends meet, the encroachment of mechanized looms threatening his craft, and the despair of obsolescence. He had led a rebellion against the machines, believing they would destroy livelihoods.

But the rebellion had failed, leading to his arrest and execution. His final thoughts were of regret—not for his actions, but for not embracing change.

Chapter Thirty-Six: Embracing Transformation

Back in his own time, Thomas awoke with a start, the book still in his lap. The experience had been more than a dream; it was a revelation.

He realized that his unease stemmed from a deep-seated fear of change—a remnant from his past life. The Industrial Revolution, with all its advancements, was a double-edged sword, and he had once been on the opposing side.

Determined to break the cycle, Thomas resolved to approach his work with empathy, considering the societal impacts of technological progress. He would advocate for the fair treatment of workers and the responsible implementation of new technologies.

The book had shown him that while innovation drives society forward, it must be balanced with compassion and foresight.

Epilogue: The Ever-Turning Wheel

The book had once again found its seeker, bridging past and present to impart timeless lessons.

As Thomas embraced his newfound purpose, the book quietly vanished, awaiting the next soul in need of its wisdom.

For in the grand tapestry of existence, each thread is connected, and the wheel of time turns unceasingly, guiding seekers toward understanding and growth.

A New Seeker in the Digital Revolution

Chapter Thirty-seven: The Programmer and the Book

Silicon Valley, USA — Year 1999

The air buzzed with anticipation as the world approached the new millennium. Emily Chen, a talented software developer, was at the forefront of the digital revolution, working tirelessly to prepare systems for the Y2K transition. The fear of the millennium bug loomed large, threatening to disrupt global infrastructures.

Late one evening, as Emily sifted through lines of code, she received an anonymous package. Inside was an unmarked, leather-bound book—a stark contrast to her digital world. Curiosity piqued, she opened it, and the room seemed to warp around her.

Chapter Thirty-eight: The Telegraph Operator's Dilemma

Emily found herself in a dimly lit room, the rhythmic clicking of a telegraph machine filling the air. She looked down to see her hands deftly tapping out messages in Morse code. The calendar on the wall read 1876.

She was now Samuel, a telegraph operator during the dawn of the telephone era. The invention of the telephone threatened to render his skills obsolete, and he faced a choice:

Embrace the new technology, learning and adapting to the changing landscape.

Cling to the familiar, resisting change and potentially facing obsolescence.

Samuel had chosen the latter, leading to a life of hardship and regret.

Chapter Thirty-nine: Embracing Change

Back in her office, Emily awoke with a start, the book resting on her desk. The experience had been more than a dream; it was a revelation.

She realized that her resistance to emerging technologies, driven by fear of the unknown, mirrored Samuel's plight. Determined not to repeat past mistakes, Emily resolved to:

Embrace new innovations, staying ahead of technological advancements.

Foster a culture of continuous learning, encouraging her team to adapt and grow.

Balance caution with curiosity, ensuring responsible development and implementation.

The book had shown her that while technology evolves, the human response to change remains constant.

Epilogue: The Ever-Turning Wheel

The book had once again found its seeker, bridging past and present to impart timeless lessons.

As Emily embraced her newfound perspective, the book quietly vanished, awaiting the next soul in need of its wisdom.

For in the grand tapestry of existence, each thread is connected, and the wheel of time turns unceasingly, guiding seekers toward understanding and growth.

Chapter forty: The Spy and the Book

Berlin, Germany — Year 1942

The city was a ghost of its former self, its streets cloaked in fear and secrecy. The world was at war, and behind every shadow lurked a whisper of betrayal. Julian Cross had learned to survive in the spaces between those whispers.

He was a British intelligence officer, embedded deep within enemy territory, masquerading as a loyal German officer. His mission was clear—uncover the

Reich's deepest secrets and ensure they never reached the battlefield.

But secrets had a way of finding him first.

One cold evening, hidden beneath the dim light of his candle lit desk, he found an unmarked package among the coded messages delivered to his safe house. It bore no insignia, no sender—only his name, scrawled in a hand that sent a chill through him.

Inside, wrapped in aged parchment, was a leather-bound book.

It was impossible. He had seen this book before, in his dreams.

Chapter Forty-One: A Life He Shouldn't Remember

The moment Julian opened the book, his vision blurred. The candlelight flickered. The walls of his safe house dissolved.

Then—he was falling.

The cold night of Berlin vanished, replaced by the roaring heat of another war.

When he hit the ground, his boots splashed in blood.

His hands gripped a sword, not a gun.

The sounds of cannon fire and muskets rang in his ears, but they did not belong to this war.

Because this was France, and the year was 1793.

Chapter Forty-Two: The Guillotine's Shadow

He stood in a crowded square, the sky grey with smoke. The air reeked of sweat, fear, and revolution. The guillotine loomed ahead, its blade sharp, dripping with the weight of history.

Julian's breath hitched. He knew this place.

Because in this life, he was not Julian Cross.

He was Étienne Beaumont, a nobleman accused of treason against the Republic. And today, he would die beneath that blade.

The memories came in sharp flashes:

A woman with piercing green eyes, whispering his name as she betrayed him to the revolutionaries.

Gold coins changing hands, sealing his fate.

His last words, spoken in defiance before they dragged him to the executioner's stage.

He had trusted her.

And she had sent him to his death.

Just as someone in his present life was about to do the same.

Chapter Forty-Three: The Message Across Time

Julian gasped, snapping back into his body. The guillotine disappeared. The French Revolution was gone.

He was back in 1942. Back in Berlin.

The book lay open before him, its pages still turning.

Sweat beaded on his brow as realization hit him. This was not just a memory. It was a warning. In his past life, he had trusted the wrong person and died for it.

And now, in this war, in this mission, history was about to repeat itself.

Someone in his network—someone he trusted—was about to betray him.

But this time...

This time, he had the book. This time, he had a chance to change the ending.

Chapter Forty-Four: The Spy's Next Move

Julian's pulse thundered as he closed the book. He no longer saw it as a relic.

It was a weapon.

A bridge between past and present, warning him of the mistakes he was doomed to repeat.

The book had saved him.

Now, he had one night to uncover the traitor before they uncovered him.

One night before the executioner's blade fell again.

And this time...

He refused to die.

Julian's Race Against Time

Chapter Forty-Five: The Web of Deceit

Berlin's streets lay under a thick veil of darkness, the oppressive silence broken only by the distant hum of military vehicles. Julian Cross, his mind still reeling from the revelations of the mysterious book, knew that every second counted. The spectre of betrayal loomed large, and he was determined to unmask the traitor before they sealed his fate.

His clandestine network within the city was vast, comprising informants, double agents, and unsuspecting civilians. Yet, the book's haunting vision had narrowed his suspicions to a select few. He meticulously reviewed recent intelligence reports, cross-referencing them with intercepted communications. Patterns began to emerge—subtle inconsistencies, delayed transmissions, and coded messages that hinted at duplicity.

One name resurfaced repeatedly: Klaus Heller, a high-ranking Abwehr officer who had recently been integrated into Julian's operations. Heller's credentials were impeccable, his loyalty ostensibly unwavering. However, the book's revelation had cast a shadow of doubt over him.

Chapter Forty-Six: The Confrontation

Under the guise of routine protocol, Julian arranged a midnight rendezvous with Heller in a secluded warehouse on the city's outskirts. The location was deliberately chosen—isolated, with no potential for eavesdropping.

As Heller arrived, his demeanour was calm, almost too composed. The two men exchanged formalities before delving into operational discussions. Julian, employing his training in psychological manipulation, subtly steered the conversation towards recent security breaches.

"It's disconcerting," Julian mused aloud, "how our enemies always seem one step ahead. Almost as if someone within our ranks is feeding them information."

Heller's eyes flickered momentarily—a barely perceptible sign, but enough to confirm Julian's suspicions.

"Do you have any leads?" Heller inquired; his voice steady but with an undertone of apprehension.

"Perhaps," Julian replied, locking eyes with him. "But trust is a fragile thing, easily shattered by betrayal."

The tension was palpable. Heller's facade began to crack, beads of sweat forming on his brow. In a swift motion, Julian drew his sidearm, aiming it squarely at Heller.

"It's over, Klaus. The game is up."

Heller's shoulders slumped, a resigned sigh escaping his lips. "You were always astute, Julian. It's a pity our paths converged this way."

Chapter Forty-Seven: The Revelation

With Heller detained, Julian delved into his personal quarters, uncovering clandestine radio equipment and cipher codes linking him directly to the enemy. Among the incriminating evidence was a photograph of Heller with a woman—the same woman from Julian's vision, the one who had betrayed him in a past life.

The realisation was staggering. The book had not only unveiled the betrayal but had also illuminated the intricate web of connections transcending time. The past and present were intertwined in a dance of fate and destiny.

Chapter Forty-Eight: The Aftermath

With the traitor exposed, Julian fortified his network, implementing stringent protocols to prevent future infiltrations. The book remained his enigmatic guide, its pages now blank, awaiting the next seeker in need of its wisdom.

As Berlin continued to smoulder under the ravages of war, Julian understood that his journey was far from over. The echoes of the past had provided clarity, but the future remains uncertain. With renewed resolve, he prepared to face the challenges ahead, knowing that the lessons of history would guide his path.

A New Seeker in the Age of Exploration

Chapter Forty-Nine: The Navigator and the Book

Lisbon, Portugal — Year 1492

The harbour of Lisbon was a tapestry of sails and masts, ships arriving and departing to the farthest reaches of the known world. The scent of saltwater mingled with exotic spices, hinting at lands beyond the horizon. Among the throng of sailors and merchants stood Isabella de Avila, a young navigator with a thirst for discovery that defied the conventions of her time.

Isabella had always felt the pull of the unknown, a magnetic attraction to the mysteries that lay beyond the mapped edges of the world. Her father, a respected cartographer, had nurtured her curiosity, teaching her the art of navigation and the science of the stars. Yet, as a woman, her aspirations were often met with scepticism and derision.

One evening, as she pored over sea charts in her modest quarters, a knock echoed through the wooden door. Opening it, she found no one—only a weathered, leather-bound book resting on the threshold. Its cover bore no title, but an inexplicable familiarity drew her to it.

Curiosity piqued, Isabella opened the book. The pages were filled with intricate illustrations of celestial maps and annotations in a script she couldn't decipher. As her fingers traced the delicate lines, a sensation of vertigo overcame her, and the room seemed to dissolve around her.

Chapter Fifty: The Viking's Voyage

When the dizziness subsided, Isabella found herself standing on the deck of a sturdy wooden ship, the chill of the northern wind biting at her skin. The crew around her spoke in a guttural language, their attire and demeanour foreign yet oddly familiar.

She realised, with a mix of awe and disbelief, that she had been transported into the body of a Viking navigator during the 9th century. The ship was part of a fleet sailing into uncharted waters, driven by a desire to discover new lands and wealth.

As days turned into weeks, Isabella—now living as the Viking navigator—experienced the exhilaration and perils of exploration. They encountered treacherous storms, navigated by the stars, and finally sighted a verdant coastline—the shores of what would later be known as Iceland.

Throughout the journey, she grappled with the challenges of leadership, the weight of decision-making, and the constant tension between ambition and responsibility. These experiences resonated deeply with her own aspirations and the obstacles she faced in her era.

Chapter Fifty-One: The Return

Abruptly, Isabella was pulled back to her own time, the familiar surroundings of her quarters materializing around her. The book lay open before her, its pages now blank, as if the ink had faded into the ether.

The vividness of the experience left her breathless. It was more than a dream; it was a revelation. The courage and determination of the Viking navigator mirrored her own desires and fears. The journey had imparted lessons that transcended time—about leadership, exploration, and the resilience needed to overcome societal constraints.

Empowered by this newfound wisdom, Isabella resolved to pursue her ambitions with renewed vigor. She would petition for a commission to lead an expedition, armed with the knowledge that the spirit of exploration was a timeless endeavour, unbound by gender or era.

The mysterious book had bridged the chasm of centuries, connecting her to a kindred spirit from the past. Its purpose fulfilled, it vanished without a trace, leaving Isabella with a profound sense of purpose and a destiny intertwined with the echoes of history.

Chapter Fifty-Two: The Philosopher's Revelation

Paris, France — Year 1775

In the heart of Paris, during a time when reason and science began to challenge long-held beliefs, lived Étienne Moreau, a philosopher deeply engrossed in the pursuit of knowledge. The city buzzed with intellectual fervour, salons filled with debates on liberty, progress, and the rights of man.

One evening, as Étienne perused ancient manuscripts in a dimly lit library, he discovered a peculiar, leather-bound book nestled among the dusty tomes. Its cover bore no title, yet it emanated an inexplicable allure. Drawn to its mystery, he opened it to find pages filled with symbols and scripts unlike any he had seen.

As he delved deeper, the room around him seemed to fade, and he was enveloped by a cascade of visions—glimpses of distant lands, unfamiliar faces, and events spanning epochs. The experience was overwhelming, yet profoundly enlightening.

Chapter Fifty-Three The Alchemist's Journey

Emerging from the visions, Étienne found himself in the body of an alchemist during the 9th century in the heart of Baghdad, the epicentre of the Islamic Golden Age. Surrounded by scholars and scientists, he was amidst a civilization that cherished knowledge and discovery.

In this new existence, Étienne, as the alchemist, engaged in experiments to transmute base metals into gold and sought the elusive elixir of life. Through his studies, he uncovered principles of chemistry and medicine far ahead of his original time. He grappled with the ethical implications of his pursuits, understanding that true enlightenment transcended material gain.

These experiences instilled in him a profound appreciation for the interconnectedness of all knowledge and the enduring quest for understanding that transcends cultures and eras.

Chapter Fifty-four: The Enlightened Path

Abruptly, Étienne was drawn back to his own time, the familiar surroundings of the Parisian library reappearing. The mysterious book lay before him, its pages now blank, as if the visions had been absorbed into his consciousness.

The journey had imparted invaluable insights. He realised that the pursuit of knowledge was a universal endeavour, unbounded by time or place. The alchemist's dedication mirrored his own, and the ethical considerations of their quests were strikingly similar.

Empowered by this revelation, Étienne dedicated himself to fostering a spirit of inquiry and openness. He began writing treatises that emphasised the unity of knowledge and the importance of ethical considerations in scientific pursuits. His works encouraged collaboration across disciplines and cultures, advocating for a holistic approach to understanding the world.

The mystical book had once again bridged time and space, guiding a seeker toward wisdom that would illuminate the path for future generations. Its purpose fulfilled, it vanished from the library, awaiting the next soul in need of its timeless guidance.

Chapter Fifty-Five: The Patriot's Awakening

Boston, Massachusetts — Year 1775

The air was thick with anticipation in the bustling port city of Boston. Tensions between the American colonies and the British Crown had reached a boiling point, and whispers of revolution echoed through the cobblestone streets. In a modest study, illuminated by the flickering glow of a solitary candle, sat Samuel Prescott, a dedicated physician and fervent patriot.

Late into the night, as Samuel pored over medical texts, a peculiar sensation washed over him. His gaze was irresistibly drawn to an unassuming, leather-bound book nestled among his collection—a book he did not recall acquiring. Its cover bore no title, yet it emanated an aura of profound significance.

Compelled by an inexplicable force, Samuel opened the book. The pages were filled with intricate diagrams and writings in a script both foreign and familiar. As his fingers traced the delicate lines, a sudden vertigo overtook him, and the room dissolved into darkness.

Chapter Fifty-Six: The Spartan's Trial

When clarity returned, Samuel found himself in an entirely different world. He stood amidst a rugged landscape, clad in bronze armour, a heavy shield strapped to his arm. The air was filled with the distant clamour of battle. He realised, with a mix of awe and trepidation, that he had assumed the identity of a Spartan warrior in ancient Greece, circa 480 BCE.

The Spartans were preparing to confront the Persian forces at the Battle of Thermopylae. As he trained and strategized alongside his fellow warriors, Samuel experienced first-hand the discipline, camaraderie, and unwavering resolve that defined Spartan society. He grappled with the harsh realities of war, the concept of sacrifice for the greater good, and the stark contrast between individual desires and collective duty.

These experiences resonated deeply with Samuel, mirroring the burgeoning revolutionary spirit in his own time. The Spartans' valour and commitment to their cause provided him with profound insights into leadership, resilience, and the complexities of freedom.

Chapter Fifty-Seven: The Midnight Ride

Abruptly, Samuel was pulled back to his own era, the familiar surroundings of his study materialising around him. The mysterious book lay open before him, its pages now blank, as if the knowledge it imparted had been absorbed into his very being.

The vividness of the experience left him breathless. It was more than a dream; it was a revelation. The lessons from his time as a Spartan warrior illuminated his path forward. He understood the importance of unity, courage, and strategic foresight in the face of overwhelming odds.

Empowered by this newfound wisdom, Samuel became more than just a physician; he emerged as a pivotal figure in the fight for independence. He joined forces with fellow patriots, including Paul Revere and William Dawes, in their daring midnight rides to warn of the approaching British forces. His actions galvanized the colonial militia, contributing to the battles of Lexington and Concord, and igniting the flames of revolution.

The enigmatic book had once again bridged time and space, imparting timeless wisdom to a seeker poised at a pivotal moment in history. Its purpose fulfilled, it vanished without a trace, awaiting the next soul in need of its guidance.

Chapter Fifty-Eight: The Guardian's Revelation

In the ethereal realm beyond the constraints of time and space, there exists a being of profound wisdom and eternal presence—the Guardian of the Book of Echoes. This ancient custodian has watched over the mystical book since its inception, ensuring that its profound knowledge reaches those destined to guide humanity toward enlightenment.

The Guardian resides in a sanctum of light and shadow, a place where the past, present, and future converge. From this vantage point, they observe the tapestry of human history, identifying pivotal moments and individuals whose actions can alter the course of destiny.

Throughout the ages, the Guardian has facilitated the Book's journey, guiding it to seekers such as Enheduanna, Hypatia, and Geoffrey Loveday. Each encounter was meticulously orchestrated to impart wisdom and inspire transformative change.

Now, as the world stands on the brink of unprecedented challenges and opportunities, the Guardian senses the emergence of a new seeker—one whose journey will intertwine with the legacy of the Book in unforeseen ways.

With a gesture, the Guardian summons the Book of Echoes, its pages shimmering with untold possibilities. The time has come to   guide the next soul, to continue the eternal mission of enlightenment and healing.

Chapter Fifty-Nine: The Awakening

In the heart of modern-day London, amidst the ceaseless hum of city life, resides Dr. Eleanor "Ellie" Thompson, a renowned neuroscientist dedicated to unravelling the mysteries of the human mind. Despite her professional success, Ellie has been plagued by recurring dreams—vivid, haunting visions of places and people she has never known, yet that feel intimately familiar.

One evening, as a torrential rain batters the city, Ellie seeks refuge in a quaint, antiquarian bookstore tucked away in a narrow alley of Bloomsbury. Drawn to a secluded corner, her eyes fall upon an unassuming, leather-bound volume—the Book of Echoes. Its cover is worn, its pages yellowed with age, yet it emanates an inexplicable allure.

Compelled by an unseen force, Ellie opens the book. As her fingers trace the faded script, a sudden wave of vertigo overwhelms her, and the world around her dissolves into darkness

Chapter Sixty: The Ancestral Memory

When Ellie regains her senses, she finds herself in a vast, open plain under a sky painted with the hues of dawn. She is no longer in London but in a prehistoric landscape, surrounded by a tribe of early humans. To her astonishment, she understands their language and customs as if they were her own.

Immersed in this ancient world, Ellie experiences life through the eyes of a young tribal healer. She learns their methods of herbal medicine, their rituals, and their deep connection to the natural world. She witnesses their joys, sorrows, and the communal bonds that hold them together.

Through these experiences, Ellie realises that the emotions and sensations she is encountering mirror the inexplicable feelings and dreams she has had in her modern life. She begins to understand that these are not mere fantasies but ancestral memories encoded within her very being.

Chapter Sixty-One: The Revelation

Abruptly, Ellie is pulled back to the present, the dim light of the bookstore coming into focus. The Book of Echoes lies open before her, its pages now blank, as if the knowledge it imparted has been absorbed into her consciousness.

The experience leaves her breathless. She comprehends that the visions she has been experiencing are ancestral memories, echoes of lives lived long ago, imprinted within her DNA. This revelation aligns seamlessly with the principles of The Loveday Method, a therapeutic approach that facilitates mental time travel to access hidden memories responsible for generational trauma.

Empowered by this newfound understanding, Ellie embarks on a journey to integrate these ancestral insights into her work. She collaborates with practitioners of The Loveday Method, bridging the gap between neuroscience and ancestral memory retrieval. Together, they develop innovative therapies to help individuals confront and heal from generational traumas, unlocking the potential for profound personal transformation.

The Book of Echoes has once again fulfilled its purpose, guiding a seeker toward enlightenment and healing. As Ellie delves deeper into her research, she becomes a beacon of hope, illustrating the profound interconnectedness of all souls and the timeless quest for self-discovery.

A Meeting Across Time

Chapter Sixty-Two: The Convergence

In the heart of Alexandria, during the height of its intellectual splendour in 370 CE, the esteemed philosopher and mathematician Hypatia delved into the mysteries of the cosmos. One evening, as she studied the stars from her observatory, a peculiar sensation enveloped her—a feeling of being both present and elsewhere.

Simultaneously, in London, Dr. Eleanor "Ellie" Thompson, a neuroscientist in 2025, sat in her laboratory, analysing neural patterns associated with ancestral memories. Suddenly, she felt a strange connection, as if her consciousness was intertwining with another's across the fabric of time.

Chapter Sixty-Three the Dialogue Beyond Time

In a realm beyond the physical, where past and present converge, Hypatia and Ellie found themselves face-to-face.

Hypatia: "Greetings, traveller. By what means have we come to share this space?"

Ellie: "I... I'm not certain. One moment I was in my lab, and now I'm here, speaking with you. You seem familiar, as if from a distant memory."

Hypatia: "Perhaps the Book of Echoes has woven our paths together. I have encountered its wisdom, guiding my studies of the heavens and the principles of mathematics."

Ellie: "The Book of Echoes... I've read about it, a mystical book connecting seekers across time. Are you... Hypatia of Alexandria?"

Hypatia: "Indeed, I am. And you, traveller, from which era do you hail?"

Ellie: "I'm Dr. Ellie Thompson, from the year 2025. I'm a neuroscientist exploring how ancestral memories influence our present selves."

Hypatia: "Fascinating. It seems the Book has bridged our times to share knowledge. Tell me, what have you discovered in your studies?"

Ellie: "I've been developing a method to help individuals access and heal generational traumas encoded in their DNA. It's called The Loveday Method."

Hypatia: "A noble pursuit. In my time, I sought to understand the cosmos and our place within it. Perhaps our endeavours are more connected than they appear."

Ellie: "I believe so. Understanding the past can illuminate our present and guide our future. Your work laid the foundations for many scientific principles we now take for granted."

Hypatia: "And your work carries forward the quest for knowledge and healing. It seems the Book of Echoes has a purpose in uniting us—to show that the pursuit of wisdom is a timeless endeavour."

Chapter Sixty-Four: The Parting Gift

As their conversation deepened, both women felt a profound connection, transcending the boundaries of time. The realm around them began to waver, signalling the end of their encounter.

Hypatia: "Ellie, take with you the understanding that knowledge is a bridge across the ages. Our efforts, though separated by centuries, are part of a continuum."

Ellie: "Thank you, Hypatia. I will carry your wisdom into my work, knowing that we are all connected in this vast tapestry of existence."

With that, the convergence faded, and both returned to their respective times, forever changed by their encounter.

The Book of Echoes,

Having traversed various eras and guided numerous seekers, sensed a pivotal moment in its existence. Recognising the need for a more structured approach to aid humanity, the book returned to its Guardian, an ancient custodian entrusted with its safekeeping and purpose.

The Guardian, a timeless entity residing in a realm beyond the constraints of ordinary time, understood the profound significance of this return. The book's journeys had illuminated individual lives, but now it sought to influence humanity on a grander scale.

In communion with the Guardian, the book revealed its intent: to become a beacon of collective wisdom, accessible to all who earnestly sought understanding and enlightenment. No longer would it appear sporadically to isolated individuals; instead, it would manifest in forms comprehensible to different cultures and societies, embedding its essence in myths, legends, and teachings across the world.

Through this transformation, the Book of Echoes aimed to inspire a universal awakening, encouraging humanity to reflect on past lessons, recognise recurring patterns, and strive towards a harmonious future. The Guardian, honouring the book's evolved purpose, released it into the currents of human consciousness, allowing its echoes to resonate through the annals of history, guiding civilizations towards wisdom and unity.

Thus, the Book of Echoes transcended its physical form, becoming an eternal whisper in the collective human psyche, ever-present and ever-guiding, as humanity continued its journey through the ages.

Ancient Mystical Book

In the heart of a tranquil village, nestled between rolling hills and ancient forests, there existed a legend of a mystical book—a book said to possess the collective wisdom of the ancients. This book, it was whispered, had the power to guide chosen individuals toward profound discoveries that could heal the deepest wounds of humanity.

One fateful night, as the village lay under a canopy of twinkling stars, a young hypnoanalyst named Geoffrey Elliot Loveday was visited by a vivid dream. In this dream, the mystical book appeared before him, its pages glowing with an ethereal light. The book spoke to him without words, imparting a profound understanding of the human mind and the hidden traumas that traverse generations.

Upon awakening, Geoffrey felt an irresistible urge to write, despite never considering himself a writer. It was as if the book had unlocked a reservoir of knowledge within him. He began to develop a method that allowed individuals to journey back through time within their minds, to confront and heal from ancestral traumas affecting their present lives.

He named this transformative approach The Loveday Method. Through it, Geoffrey guided individuals into deep trances, leading them up a symbolic staircase to a door. Upon opening this door, they would traverse back to experiences from lives long past, uncovering and addressing the root causes of their current struggles.

The objective of this mystical encounter and the subsequent development of The Loveday Method was to provide a pathway for healing—bridging the past and present, and offering individuals the opportunity to release the invisible forces of generational trauma. Geoffrey's work illuminated the profound interconnectedness of all souls and the timeless quest for self-discovery and healing.

Thus, the mystical book's wisdom found its way into the modern world through Geoffrey, guiding humanity toward a deeper understanding of itself and the eternal bonds that unite us all.

This Is Just the Beginning

As Geoffrey Elliott Loveday, a professional hypnotherapist, hypnoanalyst, and certified hypnosis instructor, I have dedicated my career to exploring the depths of the human mind and facilitating healing through innovative techniques. My journey led me to develop the Loveday Method, a therapeutic approach that emerged from a profound dream, guiding clients to relive past lives and uncover emotions affecting their present well-being.

The Loveday Method is designed to take clients on a temporal journey, allowing them to experience lives lived long before their current existence. By accessing these deep-seated memories, individuals can identify and address emotional residues that manifest as challenges in their present lives. This process not only provides insight but also facilitates profound healing, enabling clients to release burdens they may have unconsciously carried across lifetimes.

Through my work, I have witnessed the transformative power of this method, as clients gain clarity, resolve deep-rooted issues, and achieve a sense of inner peace. The narratives and journeys presented in my writings aim to illustrate the profound impact of the Loveday Method, offering readers a glimpse into the possibilities of healing and self-discovery that lie within.

For those interested in exploring this therapeutic approach further, I offer training and resources through Mindlayers, where we delve into the intricacies of the Loveday Method and its application in hypnotherapy.

The Loveday Method stands as a testament to the profound connections between our past and present selves, offering a pathway to healing that transcends time and fosters holistic well-being.

Beyond Time: The Power to Revisit, Rewrite, and Heal

Imagine a world where time is not a barrier but a gateway—a place where the past isn't just remembered, but revisited. A world where every wound, every regret, every fractured piece of the soul can be mended, not by forgetting, but by returning.

You might call it fiction, a fantasy too impossible to be true. But what if it isn't? What if the journeys I have written are more than just stories? What if time can be unravelled, re-walked, re-written—not just in history books, but in the mind itself?

Think of the pain that lingers, the echoes of moments that haunt us. Now, imagine stepping back into those very moments, not as a prisoner, but as a healer. Imagine rewriting your own past, not by changing events, but by changing how they live within you.

This is not just a story. This is a truth waiting to be uncovered. And I am here to tell you—it is real.

The Enchanted Spectacles

Once upon a time, thousands of years ago, stories were whispered to children about a pair of magical spectacles - mysterious and powerful beyond imagination. These enchanted spectacles, when worn, allowed their bearer to peer not only into the past and present but also into the future. With a single glance, they could be transported to different times and places, reliving lives they had once lived or witnessing futures yet to unfold.

It was said that these spectacles had the power to heal all the traumas of the present life by unlocking forgotten knowledge and wisdom from the past.

As the legend grew, it was believed that these spectacles could open the mind to parallel universes, revealing hidden worlds and allowing the wearer to see beyond the veil of reality. Some said the spectacles even had the power to reunite people with loved ones who had passed, bridging the gap between life and death.

These spectacles, it was said, were not crafted in this world; they came from a place beyond, a realm of infinite possibilities. Yet, as the years passed, the spectacles were lost to time, fading into myth and obscurity.

But were they truly lost? As centuries passed, humanity's understanding of the mind grew weaker, and the ancient powers we once held faded from memory. We forgot that these magical spectacles weren't merely objects; they were a symbol of the untapped potential within every human being.

Over time, we lost sight of this inner power, searching outward for solutions that could only be found within ourselves.

One night, the secret of the spectacles came to me in a dream. It wasn't the spectacles themselves that we had lost; it was the power of the mind, dormant within us all.

Through the development of The Loveday Method and Inherited Therapy, we have rediscovered how to access this ancient magic. The spectacles were never a physical artefact, but rather a way to unlock the mind's true abilities. By tapping into these forgotten depths, we can heal the wounds of the past, travel beyond the limits of time, and explore dimensions we never knew existed.

Now, the secret is unfolding. The power of the spectacles lies within each of us, waiting to be awakened. Through the mind, we can access realms beyond imagination, heal the deepest traumas, and transform our reality in ways once thought impossible.

The journey has just begun.

Chapter One: The Book of Echoes

Some books are not written. They are remembered.

There was no thunderclap, no celestial alignment, and no prophetic sign when it began. Just a quiet morning, and the weight of weariness pressing behind my eyes.

I had been searching for something I could not name - for answers, perhaps, or peace. Maybe just a sense that this life, my life, meant more than the ticking of clocks and the repetition of days. The noise of the world had grown too loud. The questions inside me are too insistent.

And then... a memory. Not mine, but somehow *of* me.

I was standing in a room that didn't exist. A child's room. Old light filtered through gauzy curtains. There was a smell - lavender and parchment. A book lay on a wooden desk, bound in worn leather, humming softly with presence. No title. No words. But I knew what it was. The Book of Echoes.

I reached for it.

The moment my fingers touched its cover, it unfolded - not just the book, but *me*. Visions spilled out; not scenes from my own life, but from those who came before me. A grandmother I had never met, crying quietly in a war-torn village. A man in robes, standing beneath stars that no longer hung in our skies. A child, barefoot and laughing, running through a field whose scent made my heart ache.

I understood, in that moment, that my life was not a single thread. It was a tapestry of inherited stories -

some whispered, some wept, some buried too deep to name.

The Book of Echoes revealed them not as burdens, but as *bridges*. They were connections - to those who came before, to those who might come after. Their pain lived in my body. Their joy echoed in my heartbeat. Their choices shaped the unseen corners of my mind.

And I had never been taught to listen. But now, I did.

That dream - if it was a dream - stayed with me for weeks. I began to wake up with fragments of other lives at the edge of my consciousness. Names I didn't recognise. Emotions that weren't mine, yet felt intimately familiar. My sleep deepened. My waking mind grew restless.

This was when I began to shape what would become *The Loveday Method* - a way to trace the echoes through the body and soul, gently uncovering the inherited memories that had settled like dust in the corners of our psyche. Memories passed through bloodlines. Through culture. Through silence.

It was not a method born from theory. It was born from need. From the aching desire to feel whole again.

And the spectacles? They returned.

Not physically. Not yet. But I began to *see* differently.

I could look at an old photo and feel the sorrow stitched into the smile of the person posing. I could hear a certain song and be transported - not just to a memory, but to a moment in someone else's life that lived in me. A heartbeat from the past echoing through my present.

The spectacles weren't glasses. They were perceptions.

A state of attunement to the unseen layers of existence. A reawakening of the mind's most ancient gift; the ability to see beyond time.

With each session of the Loveday Method, I found myself guiding others through their own echoes. We cried the tears of their great-grandmothers. We unlocked grief trapped in the hips, stories coiled in the shoulders, voices silenced in the throat.

And healing happened. Real, visceral healing. Not just for the individual, but across timelines. Across generations.

This is why I believe the spectacles were never truly lost. They live in every one of us. They are not tools. They are a *remembrance*.

And *The Book of Echoes* - the one I found in that dream, in that place beyond time - was not given to me alone.

It is written by each of us, waiting to be read.

Chapter Two: Remembering the Spectacles

What you seek is not lost - it is simply waiting to be seen differently.

- ***G E Loveday***

I didn't set out to find the spectacles.

I didn't even believe they were real - at least, not in the way old stories describe; polished lenses made of crystal and starlight, frames humming with ancient energy, a relic from some forgotten realm.

No, when the spectacles returned to me, they came first as a *feeling* - a subtle shift in perception. Like standing in a familiar room and suddenly noticing a door that had always been there, just hidden in the wallpaper's pattern.

It started slowly.

Colours became more vivid. The space between seconds seemed to stretch. I'd catch myself staring into the distance, sensing movement in places where there was none. Time became... soft. Malleable. Moments from childhood overlapped with dreams I hadn't yet had. It was disorienting at first - like remembering something before it had even happened.

That was when I realised: I wasn't remembering the spectacles. The spectacles were remembering me.

As children, we saw the world with these eyes. Wide open. Imaginative. Undiluted by logic or linearity. We didn't just play pretend - we *knew*. We knew there were other worlds. We felt our ancestors watching over us.

We saw the shimmer in the air when someone spoke from their soul.

But we grew up. We closed the door.

The spectacles were never lost. They were packed away with our childhood drawings and dreams. Covered by layers of rationality, trauma, and distraction. We stopped looking inward. We stopped listening.

And yet, the spectacles wait patiently. Because they are not outside of us. They are a state of *being*.

To remember the spectacles is to remember yourself - your full self, unfragmented by time or pain. It is to see with the eyes of the soul. To hold the past, present, and future in the palm of one breath. It is to feel the presence of the unseen and know it as truth.

When the spectacles first reactivated in me, I would have flashes - moments that didn't belong to my linear life.

I saw myself in a different body, walking along a cliff's edge, wind in my hair that wasn't mine. I heard a voice call my name in a language I'd never learned, but somehow understood. I felt grief for someone I had never met - yet missed as if they had died only yesterday.

At first, I questioned my sanity. But then I remembered the Book of Echoes, and I began to *listen*. Not with my ears - but with my awareness. And slowly, the fragments began to form a constellation. They weren't hallucinations. They were *truths*, surfacing after generations of forgetting.

The spectacles weren't a tool I used. They were the way I *became*.

By this time, The Loveday Method had already begun to take shape.

At its heart, it is not a healing technique. It is a *remembering technique*.

A way of guiding people back into their own inner seeing. Not through force or fixing, but through softness - through the sacred act of attention.

Through breathing work, gentle inquiry, embodied awareness, and ancestral resonance, we began to coax open the locked doors of memory. And when the door opened - when the spectacles clicked into place - the results were staggering.

People reported visions of past lives. Encounters with departed loved ones. Sudden insights into why they carried pain in certain parts of their bodies. Or why certain relationships felt older than time.

They weren't imagining. They were remembering. And in remembering, the healing began.

The spectacles are not meant to shield the eyes. They are meant to unveil the soul.

They don't show you a different world. They reveal the *whole* world - the threads of truth, energy, ancestry, and eternity that have always been woven into your life.

We are each born with them. We simply forget how to wear them.

But now, the world is changing. The old knowledge is returning. And the dream is no longer confined to sleep.

If you're holding this book, something in you is already remembering.

I awoke with tears on my face. Not from sadness, but from recognition. The kind of tears you cry when something ancient within you finally exhales. When a truth you've carried silently for lifetimes is spoken aloud - without words.

The spectacles weren't placed on my face in the dream. They *became* my eyes.

I saw through time. Not like a film reel or a vision, but as if all moments were layered over each other, transparent and humming - like pages of a manuscript written on glass. I could walk into the memory of my mother's grief before I was born. I could feel the laughter of a child I hadn't yet met. I could hear the soft songs of ancestors I never knew I longed for.

The dream didn't end. It simply changed shape. When I opened my eyes, the world was the same. But I was not.

The walls of my room seemed to pulse with quiet knowing. The light through the window carried something... more. And beneath the rhythm of my own heartbeat was a new pulse - ancient, steady, echoing like footsteps down a hallway I'd forgotten existed.

That morning, I began to write - not from the mind, but from the space behind it. The Loveday Method spilled out like a remembered language. I wasn't inventing it. I was *translating* it.

A practice for those ready to listen inward. To retrieve the stories that live not in books, but in the body. To unlock the inherited memories woven into our DNA, our dreams, our daily reactions.

It begins quietly. Always.

A flash of emotion you can't explain. A repetitive dream. A deep knowing that certain pains don't belong to *you*, yet live inside you all the same.

And this is where the Book of Echoes whispers, *"Begin here."*

It's never about fixing. It's about *remembering*. Not about going back, but going *through*.

Each person I've worked with has carried their own hidden library - ancestral pages waiting to be turned. I've seen people remember lifetimes in a single breath. I held hands as someone met the unspoken grief of a great-grandmother who lost her child and never spoke of it, but passed that ache through the bloodline like a shadow no one could name.

And when that echo is finally heard - when the story is seen and honoured - something miraculous happens.

The body exhales.

The nervous system softens.

The chain breaks.

And the spectacles? They return for them too.

Sometimes slowly - through meditation, dreams, flashes of knowing. Sometimes all at once - with visions, past-life recall, waves of ancestral presence. But always, the same truth becomes clear.

What we thought was magic, was memory. What we thought was lost, was simply waiting.

And so, the work continues. Quietly. Reverently. Not to build a new path, but to clear away what covers the ancient one beneath our feet.

We are not creating the way. We are *remembering* it.

The Book of Echoes lives in all of us. The spectacles are already yours. You need only learn to see with them again.

Chapter Three: Through the Veil

To see through the veil is to live in two worlds at once - and to walk them both with grace.

There is a moment - small and easily missed - when the veil between worlds thins. Not in the pages of legend, but in the quiet pulse of daily life.

You're stirring your tea, watching the leaves settle, and suddenly it feels like someone is watching you. Not in fear, but in familiarity. You glance toward the window and catch a flicker of movement, though no one is there. You hear a whisper in your mind that feels like it came from someone else's memory.

These moments are not hallucinations. They are intersections. This is what it means to begin living *through* the veil.

We are not taught to trust these sensations. The world of logic tells us they are meaningless - coincidence, tricks of the mind. But when you wear the spectacles - when you let them adjust your inner lens - you begin to understand that reality is layered.

There is the physical world. The tangible. The measurable.

And then there is the subtle world. The energetic. They remembered the feeling.

When the veil thins, you don't stop living your "normal" life. You still make coffee. You still go to work. You still pay bills. But you begin to *feel* everything differently.

Words carry more weight. Rooms carry more stories. Even your own body becomes a living archive - holding echoes in the tightness of a shoulder, the warmth of a touch, the ache of an old wound that doesn't seem to belong to your timeline

One woman I worked with described it like this:

"It's like the air is more alive. I don't see ghosts. But I feel presence. I feel history. I touch a tree and I remember a version of me who once lived in a forest. I walk into my childhood home and finally understand that the fear I felt wasn't mine - it belonged to my father's father, and it lived in the wallpaper. I can't explain it. But I know it's real."

These are the moments when the veil grows thin. And when it does, the spectacles allow you not to run - but to listen.

You begin to *read* the world the way you read the Book of Echoes.

Everything becomes a message. A memory. A mirror.

At first, it can feel like too much. The floodgates open. You *see* too much. You *feel* too much.

This is where practice and presence become vital. The spectacles may reveal many doors - but it is your choice which ones you walk through.

Not every memory must be relived. Not every echo must be chased. Healing is not about drowning in the past - it is about integrating what rises, and carrying it with compassion into the now.

You do not become less human when you wear the spectacles. You become *more*.

More attuned. More embodied. More aware of the sacredness pulsing beneath the mundane.

You begin to walk as a bridge - between timelines, between lives, between the known and the unknowable.

And in doing so, you become the living veil. The seen and the unseen. The past, the present, and the possibility.

Chapter Four: The Girl Who Remembered Fire

Some memories are not yours - but they are waiting for you just the same.

Her name was Sarah.

She came to me during the winter months, when the nights were longest and the veil seemed to hover just above the skin. She was quiet at first. Wary. Not broken - but holding herself in pieces, as if her presence in the world came with conditions.

There was something in her eyes. A deep ache wrapped in curiosity. She didn't come for healing. She came for answers.

"I don't know why," she said, her voice barely louder than the hum of the heater. "But I keep having dreams of fire. Always fire. Sometimes I'm watching it from far away. Sometimes I'm in it. Sometimes I am it."

The dreams had followed her since childhood. Her family brushed it off - nightmares, anxiety, and imagination. But the fire persisted. It didn't burn her skin. It burned her memory.

She began to feel it even while awake - heat in her palms, sudden flashes of smoke that weren't there, the taste of ash on her tongue when she was completely alone.

Sarah hadn't come looking for spectacles. But they had already started to return to her.

The First Session

We began gently - with breathing, grounding, and presence. I explained that we would not "go searching" for answers, but rather allow them to rise on their own. That's what the spectacles require - a stillness, a receptivity, a trust.

She lay back, eyes closed. I guided her to the place I call "the in-between" - not quite a dream, not quite memory, but a space where echoes rise and time softens.

Within minutes, her breath changed.

"There's a girl," she whispered. "She's hiding in a root cellar. She's maybe nine. Her hands are dirty. There's smoke in the air. She's... she's waiting to be burned."

Tears came - sudden and visceral. Not from fear, but from recognition.

"They're going to burn her. They think she's a witch. But she's just... different. She sees things. She speaks of stars and spirits and plants that heal. They don't understand her. They think she's dangerous."

Sarah began to tremble.

I stayed close, grounded in stillness, holding space for what surfaced - not trying to fix it, only to witness.

And then came the shift.

"Wait... she's not afraid anymore. She's rising. She's stepping into the fire."

Sarah's face softened.

"She's not dying. She's becoming. She's turning to light. She's showing me that I'm not supposed to run from the fire. I'm supposed to remember it."

And just like that, something ancient broke free.

When the session ended, Sarah looked as if she had returned from another world.

Because she had.

Over the next few weeks, things began to change. Sarah no longer feared the fire. In fact, she welcomed it.

She began to see its symbolism in her life - how she had always held herself back out of fear of being "too much," too intense, too intuitive, too unexplainable. She realised the echoes of that old life were still shaping her decisions today.

She began drawing again - images of stars, flames, women rising from ash. She uncovered a family line of herbalists, midwives, and intuitive women - most of whom had their histories scrubbed clean by silence.

"I thought I was broken," she told me. "But I was just remembering something I didn't know I was allowed to remember."

The spectacles had revealed her lineage. Not in documents or names, but in feeling. In knowing. In the sacred clarity of seeing through the veil.

Sarah's story is one of many.

Each person who reclaims the spectacles does so in their own way. For some, it is a dream. For others, a pain in the body that speaks in metaphor. For many, it is the slow unwrapping of silence passed down through generations.

But in each case, the pattern is the same:

The veil thins.

The memory rises.

The soul remembers.

The present transforms.

This is the power of the spectacles. Not as magic - but as memory. Not as fantasy - but as permission.

To remember who you've always been. To reclaim what you were taught to fear. To see fire not as destruction - but as the beginning of light.

Chapter Five: The Boy Who Dreamed in Futures

Not all echoes come from the past. Some arrive ahead of their time, calling you forward.

His name was Elliott.

He was only seventeen when I first met him - sharp, quiet, and carrying an exhaustion that felt too old for his years. He had the posture of someone who was always listening - head slightly tilted, eyes constantly scanning the horizon for something no one else could see.

Elliott didn't speak much at first. Not out of shyness, but from a deep, silent reverence. As if he knew the world he walked through was not the only one that existed.

"I don't dream like other people," he said eventually, his fingers curled around the rim of a chipped mug. "I don't see the past. I see what hasn't happened yet. People I haven't met. Places I've never been. Conversations I swear I've already had... but not yet."

He told me he'd wake up with blueprints in his head. Visions of cities that hadn't been built. Languages with grammar he somehow understood. Once, he described a healing technology made entirely of sound and light.

He wasn't afraid of it. But he felt... *disoriented*. Like his soul had skipped ahead and was calling back to him through time.

This, too, is the gift of the spectacles. Time doesn't always move forward.

While Sarah's memories revealed the past, Elliott's connection was rooted in the future.

This is something rarely spoken of in traditional healing. We often focus on what's behind us - trauma, lineage, loss. But there are also futures encoded in our DNA. Visions passed down from ancestors not as burdens, but as *seeds*. The soul doesn't only carry pain. It carries possibility.

And sometimes, those possibilities arrive early.

With Elliott, the work was less about healing the old and more about anchoring the new.

Our first session was different.

Elliott didn't close his eyes. He kept them open, watching a point just beyond my shoulder, as if someone else were in the room, guiding him. His voice was steady, almost detached, like he was reading from a script written in stardust.

"There's a building made of water," he whispered. "It vibrates. People walk through it, and it heals them. Not just physically - emotionally. Their memories rearrange. Their grief dissolves. And then... they remember who they really are."

He stopped and blinked, like waking from a trance.

"I don't know where that is. But I've been there. I've seen myself there. Working. Teaching. It hasn't happened yet... but it *will*."

We didn't need to interpret. We simply let it be.

Because that's the other side of the spectacles: Not all remembering is backward. Some are forward - reaching into the soul's contract, the future-self echoing back, calling us to rise.

Elliott began to change after that. He stopped calling himself strange. He stopped trying to silence his knowing. Instead, he began *tracking* it.

He kept a journal - not of what had happened, but what *would*. Symbols, sketches, fragments of phrases that made no sense to anyone but him. And over time, those fragments began to align with things in the waking world.

He met a teacher from a country he'd drawn in childhood. He discovered a real sound therapy method almost identical to what he'd dreamt years earlier. He began studying quantum biology. Frequencies. Time.

He wasn't becoming someone new. He was *remembering* who he was meant to become.

The spectacles don't always show us the past. Sometimes, they let us remember *forward* - pulling through timelines not yet walked but already written in the soul.

Elliott taught me that future-memories are just as sacred as ancestral ones. That our purpose often whispers long before we are ready to understand it. And that remembering the future can be just as healing as recovering the past.

This, too, is the work. This, too, is the journey. Not to predict the future. But to align with it.

To live in such resonance with your soul's design that the path reveals itself one breath at a time.

Chapter Six: The Woman Who Carried the Ache

Sometimes the body remembers what the mind has forgotten.

Her name was Shanna. She arrived not seeking answers, but relief. The first thing she said to me was:

When I met her, Shanna was in the early stages of what she called a "slow love." She had met someone kind, gentle, patient - a man named Julian who asked all the right questions and gave her all the time she needed. And yet, every time she let him near, her body reacted with fear.

Tension. Resistance. Pain. As if her body didn't trust what her heart wanted.

She wasn't afraid of Julian. She was afraid of something *beneath* him. Something that hadn't yet surfaced.

And that's where the spectacles began to stir. Not in her dreams. Not in visions. But in her spine.

A Different Kind of Session:

When we began, I asked her not what she remembered - but what she *felt*.

She closed her eyes. Her breath slowed. She placed one hand on the base of her back.

"It's like a stone," she said. "Heavy. But familiar. Like I've carried it a long time. Even before this life."

As we dropped deeper, her body began to tremble.

Memories surfaced - not in perfect clarity, but as sensations, symbols, flashes of colour and sound.

"There's a woman," she whispered. "She's hunched over, clutching her belly. She's lost someone. A child. A lover. Maybe both. She's waiting for someone to come back, but they never do."

The grief that followed was oceanic. Her breath came in waves. Her hands clenched. Tears rose and fell in silence.

And then, a whisper:

"She never let anyone close again. Not really. She closed her body like a door. And the door never reopened."

In the days after the session, something shifted in Shanna. The pain didn't vanish instantly. But it began to move. To speak.

She realised that whenever Julian touched her in kindness, it activated the echo of abandonment from another time. Her body didn't fear *him*. It feared loss. The kind that comes after trust. The kind you don't survive twice.

But now, she was beginning to see differently.

The spectacles had turned inward - illuminating the scar not just in her heart, but in her very tissue. She began to respond to the pain not with frustration, but with reverence. To see it as an echo. A messenger. A relic of love lost and withheld.

And slowly, she began to let him in. Not all at once. But with awareness. With presence. Each moment of softness became a small ceremony of return.

We often speak of healing as an individual journey. But Shanna taught me that sometimes, the key is another person.

Julian didn't "fix" her. He *held* her - gently, steadily - while she found the courage to see herself again.

This is also the work of the spectacles.

They don't just show you memories. They show you *why* you've been guarding them. They show you how love can reopen the doors we locked lifetimes ago.

The body is a storyteller.

Shanna's healing was not linear. There were setbacks. Surges. Quiet nights when the ache returned. But over time, she stopped fearing the pain. She began listening to it.

She began tracing the shape of the story written in her body - and allowing Julian to read it with her, line by line.

And one night, months later, she sent me a message:

"The pain is gone. Not because I got rid of it, but because I finally met the part of me that created it. And she no longer needs to protect me."

This is what happens when the spectacles are worn through the skin. When memory lives in muscle, and healing comes not from insight - but from *allowing love to touch what we thought was untouchable.*

Chapter Seven: The Child Who Spoke in Stars

Some souls are born remembering.

His name was John.

He was only six when his mother brought him to me - wide-eyed, quiet, and impossibly still for someone so small. There was a gentleness about him, not timid, but ancient. As though he carried the weight of a wisdom too large for his frame.

His mother, Jane, had tears in her eyes the moment we sat down.

"He's always talking about things that don't make sense," she said. "He tells me I'm not my real name. That he used to be my brother. He hums songs he's never heard before and stares at the sky for hours. He's not troubled, just... different. And I feel like I'm losing him to something I can't understand."

I knelt to meet John's gaze.

He looked at me without flinching. Not a flicker of discomfort. Only recognition.

"You remember," he said simply. "Like me." John didn't need a session. He was *in* a session.

The moment he entered the room, the atmosphere shifted. Time slowed. The space between words grew softer, more alive. He walked to the window and traced constellations on the glass, whispering names I didn't recognise.

"They're waiting," he said. "They said you'd help Mama remember her promise."

Jane paled.

"He says I made a soul promise before he was born. That I'd help him find something he left behind in another life."

She laughed nervously, tears close to the surface.

"I was raised Catholic. I don't even know if I believe in any of this. But when he talks like that, I *feel* something. Like I've forgotten something I promised to remember."

John turned from the window.

"It's okay," he said. "I remember for both of us."

Most of us forget. We grow older. We become efficient. Logical. Measured. We trade intuition for information, dreams for deadlines, inner vision for eyesight.

But some children - like John - still wear the spectacles.

They're born with them intact. Not as a gift, but as a natural state of being. They haven't yet been talked out of their knowledge. They haven't yet learned not to believe themselves.

John remembered things he had no way of learning. The taste of a country he had never visited. The grief of a sister he never met. He described events from his mother's childhood with eerie precision - things even she had forgotten until he spoke them aloud.

"He told me about a swing tied to the apple tree at my grandmother's house," Jane whispered once. "I haven't been there in decades. I didn't even remember it myself until he described it - down to the colour of the rope."

With John, there was no need for guidance. He didn't need to *find* the spectacles. He was the reminder that they had never been lost.

He became a teacher.

He told me that children dream more vividly because they haven't been closed yet. That crying for no reason is usually remembering something too big for words. That adults lose their way when they stop listening to the wind, the trees, and the space between their own thoughts.

And then, one day, he said something I will never forget:

"The reason I came back was to help Mama open her eyes again. Not these ones" - he pointed to his face - "but the real ones. The ones in here." He placed his hand gently over his heart.

Jane's journey didn't come in visions or deep sessions. It came in *watching* her son live as if the veil didn't exist.

She began meditating - not to escape, but to listen. She found herself dreaming more. She started painting again, something she hadn't done since she was fifteen. And with each brushstroke, she felt closer to the girl she used to be - before she'd traded imagination for responsibility.

"He's helping me remember who I was before the world told me who to be," she said one afternoon.

And that, perhaps, is the greatest medicine the spectacles offer. Not just to see what was or what will be - but to *become* again.

To return to the natural state of wonder. Of presence. Of play.

John reminded me that some of our greatest teachers arrive small. That the veil is thinnest in childhood. And that sometimes, we're not meant to teach the next generation.

We're meant to *remember through them*. The spectacles live most clearly in the eyes of those who haven't yet learned to doubt them.

And if we listen closely - truly, humbly listen - they might just remind us how to see again.

Chapter Eight: The Man Who Remembered at the End

Some memories wait until the heart is quiet enough to hear them.

His name was Walter.

He was eighty-three when we met. Sceptical, sharp-witted, and more curious than he'd ever admit. He walked into the session room like a man who had nothing left to prove - just a quiet question lodged beneath his ribs.

"I don't know why I'm here," he said flatly. "I've lived a long life. I've seen wars and weddings, funerals and fireworks. But lately, I keep waking up with a woman's name in my mouth. A name I've never said aloud. And when I say it, I cry. I don't know her. But I *miss* her."

That was all it took. The spectacles had already begun to return.

Walter wasn't a man of dreams or mysticism. He believed in concrete things. Wood you could carve. Soil you could plant. Hands you could hold. But something had begun to shift in him.

He spoke of waking in the night to music he couldn't place - old, haunting, from no radio or memory. He'd sit up in bed, hand to chest, eyes brimming with tears, unable to explain what he was mourning.

"It feels like I left something unfinished. But not in this life. Somewhere else. Someone else."

And then, without prompting, he added:

"Do you believe in more than one life?"

I told him the truth.

"I believe we leave breadcrumbs across timelines. Sometimes, the soul circles back to gather what was left behind."

He nodded, slowly.

"Then I think I'm here to pick something up."

In our first session, Walter didn't close his eyes. He sat in silence, breathing steadily, one hand resting over his heart.

"Her name is Alina," he said.

He didn't know where it came from. It wasn't anyone he'd known. But he spoke it like a prayer. Like a wound.

As we moved gently through his memory - past the expected moments, past the family stories and the griefs he *did* understand - another world began to stir beneath the surface.

He described a shoreline he had never visited. A field of wild violets. A wooden boat carved by hand.

"She wore her hair braided with thread," he said suddenly. "Gold thread. I can feel the braid in my fingers."

He paused, then whispered: "She died young. I never got to say goodbye."

Walter didn't weep like a child. He wept like a man who had held something sacred inside for far too long.

He didn't need a full past-life regression. He didn't need every detail filled in.

The memory came in essence, not in facts. In texture. In emotion. In knowing. And it was enough.

Enough to soften a hardness he hadn't known he'd built. Enough to forgive himself for something he couldn't name but had carried for decades. Enough to feel - truly feel - for the first time in years.

"I didn't know you could grieve for someone who wasn't from this lifetime," he said quietly.

And I replied: "You can. Because love doesn't live in time."

Not all awakenings come in youth. Not all visions appear in dreams. Some arrive like the turning of the tide - quiet, undeniable, unstoppable.

Walter reminded me that the spectacles often choose their moment. And when they come late, they come *pure*.

There's no need to perform. No desire to dramatize. Only the truth. Only remembrance.

Before he left, Walter sat with me in silence for a long while.

Then he said: "I thought my life was winding down. But now I feel like something is *just* beginning."

He smiled, a little embarrassed.

"Maybe I'll see her again. When I go. Maybe she's the one who sent me here."

He stood up slowly, pressed a hand to my shoulder, and added; "Thank you. Not for the healing. For the remembering."

Walter passed away just under a year later.

His daughter wrote to tell me he'd been at peace in those final months. That he'd begun writing again. Telling stories to his grandchildren about "a girl with gold in her hair." That he laughed more. Rested better. Loved deeper.

She said; "It was like something he'd been waiting for finally came home to him."

And maybe that's what the spectacles do best. Not just help us see what's gone, or what's coming – but to bring us *home* to what we've always carried. Even if it takes a lifetime to remember.

Chapter Nine: The Woman Who Tried to Forget

Sometimes, remembering begins with resistance.

Her name was Nina. And Nina did not believe in any of this.

She arrived with folded arms, narrowed eyes, and a tone that said, *"I'm not here for magic - I'm here because my sister made me come."*

"Just so we're clear," she said, not even sitting down yet, "I don't buy into past lives or soul contracts or spirit guides or whatever this is. I just want to sleep again."

Insomnia had plagued her for nearly two years - waking every night at 3:33 AM with her heart pounding, soaked in sweat, sometimes with tears already on her cheeks.

"I don't even remember the dreams," she admitted. "But I wake up feeling... haunted. Like something's trying to break through. It's exhausting."

She paused. "And it's starting to scare me."

That was the crack in the armour. Not belief. Not curiosity. Just *weariness*. And maybe, a little hope.

Sometimes, the spectacles don't awaken gently.

Sometimes, they rattle the walls. Disturb your sleep. Break down the carefully constructed world you've used to protect yourself from the deeper truth.

And Nina had built a fortress.

Her life was organised, efficient, and rational. She was successful. Grounded. Busy. And yet - underneath it all - was a subtle vibration of grief. One she couldn't place.

"I'm fine," she said more than once. But her body told another story.

On our third session - after nearly two hours of rational deflection, questions, and uneasy silence - something finally cracked.

It wasn't a vision. It wasn't a memory. It was a sound. A single note on a Tibetan singing bowl. Low. Steady. Resonant.

And Nina - eyes wide, breath caught – whispered; "That sound... I know that sound."

She began to cry without warning. Her hands trembled. She curled into herself like a child.

"There was a bell. A temple. Stone walls. I was hiding... someone was coming. I wasn't allowed to speak. I wasn't allowed to *be*."

And then, the phrase that unlocked it all; "I chose to forget. I made myself forget. That's why it's been so loud inside me."

Not everyone forgets by accident. Some of us *choose* to forget. To survive. To adapt. To stay safe.

Nina had once lived a life where her voice cost her everything. A teacher. A seer. A threat to those in power.

She had been silenced - and in the deepest part of her soul, she had vowed:

"Never again."

That vow echoed into her current life.

She had built an identity around stability, logic, control. And yet the soul - the eternal keeper of memory - never stopped whispering.

The spectacles didn't force her to remember. They simply waited, patiently, until she was ready to see again.

Over time, Nina began to soften.

She still rolled her eyes when I used words like "timeline" or "soul contract." But she no longer dismissed the way her body reacted to certain sounds, places, or emotions.

She began to listen to her dreams, even if she didn't understand them. She started singing again - just to herself, in quiet places. She lit candles at night, without knowing why, and whispered the name she remembered in that first session.

Not as an answer. But as a reunion.

Nina's healing didn't come from believing in the spectacles.

It came from *surrendering* to what her body already knew. From letting her soul out of its cage.

And eventually, she said something I'll never forget; "I still don't know if I believe in all this... but I believe in *me* now. And that's new."

That is the power of the spectacles. Not to convince. But to invite. To create enough stillness, enough honesty, enough space - for remembering to arise on its own.

Not everyone walks into this work ready to remember. Some come clenching their fists. But even that is a form of reverence.

Resistance is often the soul's final defence… before it opens. And when it does?

What we find beneath it is rarely fragile. It is *fire*. It is *truth*. It is *us*, unforgotten.

Chapter Ten: The First Remembering

Long before time kept clocks, we were seen.

Before there were names, there were vibrations. Before there were words, there was knowing. And before we forgot, we were given a gift.

The Enchanted Spectacles were not made. They were *given*.

And they were not glasses. Not really. They were a transmission - a living code carried by starlight and soul-light, seeded by the Ancients who remembered us before we knew ourselves.

This is the part of the story that doesn't begin on Earth.

They were called many things in many cultures - The Watchers, The Rememberers, and The Keepers of the Golden Thread. Not gods, not aliens, not spirits, but *Bridgers*; beings who walked freely between dimensions of thought, matter, and soul.

They did not create humanity. They *saw* us. In our fire, our fear, our endless becoming.

And when they looked upon our timeline, they wept - not from pity, but from love. They saw the pain that would come. The forgetting. The violence of separation. The long, lonely journey we would take... away from ourselves.

And so, they offered something. Not to stop the forgetting - but to promise the remembering.

A *seed*. A symbol. A sensory key woven into the architecture of our souls.

The Enchanted Spectacles.

They knew forgetting would be necessary. The soul craves experience. Challenge. Story.

But they also knew that we'd reach a tipping point - a time when the pain of forgetting would outweigh the purpose.

And in that moment, the spectacles would activate. Not as objects, but as *invitations*.

The covenant was simple:

"When they are ready, let them see. Let the pain guide them back, not destroy them. Let the memory return, piece by piece, through breath, through body, through dream."

And so they encoded the spectacles in us.

In our DNA. In our myths. In the hidden spaces between music and silence, grief and joy.

They placed them in the stories that survive fires. In lullabies passed down without knowing. In the ache behind your ribs when you look at the stars and *almost* remember something.

They made the spectacles invisible - so that only those who truly *seek* would find them.

Not because the ancients wanted to test us. But because the sacred must always be chosen.

The spectacles were a promise. A promise that forgetting would never be forever. That when we were ready - truly ready - the doors would swing open again.

And so they waited.

Throughout the ages, they waited. Through wars and wonders. Through the rise and fall of empires and civilizations. They waited. Watching for the light to flicker back on in the human mind.

And now, it has begun.

Remembering is awakening across the globe. In therapists and teachers. In children and elders. In those who dream, and those who create, and those who have finally grown tired of suffering in silence.

The spectacles are humming. The ancient agreement is activating. You are reading this not by accident. You are here because *you were part of the promise.*

You chose to forget. And now... you're choosing to see.

Chapter Eleven: The One Who Saw Through the Flame

Initiation never arrives politely. It comes to burn what you're not meant to carry forward.

Her name was Gema.

And when she came to me, she wasn't searching for healing. She was searching for survival.

It was late autumn, the trees half-bare, and the wind biting through the air like a whisper of something ancient. She showed up on the third day of a three-day retreat - the final day - having driven for five hours in silence, not even knowing why she came.

She arrived with the look of someone just barely holding it together. Her hands shook as she poured her tea. Her voice was distant.

"Something's breaking open in me," she said. "But I don't know if I'm ready for what's on the other side."

Gema had spent most of her life being the "strong one." A clinical psychologist. A crisis responder. Trained in every model of trauma work - but now unravelling under the weight of her own unprocessed grief.

"It started with nightmares," she whispered. "Then the waking visions. Then the voices - not scary ones, but... ancient ones. Kind and knowing. But all too familiar."

She had tried every tool she trusted. Nothing touched it. That's when she found a recording of The Loveday Method.

She told me she felt like something in her spine clicked when she heard it. Not the words. The *frequency.*

"It was like I was being remembered by something I didn't know I'd forgotten."

And then came the fire. It wasn't a formal ritual. There were no feathers, no smoke, no circle of sacred women drumming beneath the moon.

It was just her. Alone. Wrapped in a blanket. Eyes wide open. And something... *opened.*

She later described it like this; "The ground dissolved. I wasn't sitting anymore. I was falling; through time. Through memories that weren't mine. Through lives I didn't live - but *did.*

There was a desert. A temple. I was dressed in white, standing before a crowd with a flame in my palm. I was teaching. *Healing.* But then came the silence. The stone walls. The betrayal. The burning."

She screamed - but not from fear. From *knowing.* From release. From the moment the spectacles descended upon her - not as glass, but as flame - she saw everything.

Her past lives. Her unspoken lineage. Her role in ancient orders. The vows she made to never speak again. The day she promised to hide her magic.

"It was all still there," she wept later. "Every vow, every wound, every gift. And the spectacles... they didn't just let me see. They *demanded* I remember."

As the ceremony moved through her, something in the core of The Loveday Method came alive - its original design.

It had always been more than just breath-work and ancestral mapping. It was a resonance technology passed through time. A multidimensional key embedded in our cells.

The Method doesn't just help you remember your past. It helps you *burn through* the blocks that were built to keep you from yourself.

And for Gema, the flame was the only thing strong enough to melt the armour.

"The Loveday Method didn't show me what was broken," she told me later. "It showed me what was *waiting.*"

She emerged hours later, barefoot and wide-eyed. The yurt was silent. The air smelled like myrrh and old stone. She walked like a woman who had remembered fire. Like someone who could now wield it.

And the first thing she said was: "I don't think the spectacles were ever lost."

She smiled through her tears, "I think we just stopped believing we were worthy of seeing."

For some, the spectacles arrive in dreams. For others, in grief. For Gema - they arrived the moment she finally stopped running from her soul.

Not everyone needs a ceremony. But some souls, some wounds, some gifts… they need fire. They need a moment so undeniable, so soul-shaking, that you can't go back. You *won't* go back.

Because now, you've seen what you *are*, and you'll never again be content pretending otherwise.

The spectacles will find you. In crisis. In creation. In the space between breaths. And when they do, you'll know.

Because everything will burn - and only the truth will remain.

Chapter Twelve: The Man Who Fell Through the Sky

Some awakenings do not arrive gently - they tear you from time, and return you changed.

His name was Caleb.

A seasoned mountaineer, grounded and earth-bound. Built for logic and grit. He had survived avalanches, rockslides, and months alone in the Himalayas. He trusted in instinct, not imagination.

But what happened on a solo climb in Norway shattered every known law he'd built his life upon.

He wasn't searching for answers. He wasn't healing from trauma. He just wanted the silence of the ice.

"I went to clear my head," Caleb said. "I didn't expect to fall through the sky."

It happened fast. A misstep. A sheet of black ice. A plunge off a cliff that should have ended in shattered bone and darkness.

But instead of impact, there was... *nothing*.

"I never hit the ground. I fell, but then... I wasn't falling. I was *suspended*."

He found himself inside something he couldn't describe - a space that felt both infinite and intimately alive. No sound. No time. Just light - thick, golden, and humming.

"I wasn't alone. Something was there. Watching. Waiting. It didn't speak with words, but I understood everything it said."

And then, the light shifted.

Two glowing rings began to rotate in front of him, pulsing with symbols that defied logic - ancient, galactic, human and not. They hovered like living entities, vibrating with a strange intelligence.

"They weren't glasses. They were *codes*. Spiralling. Calling. When they moved over my eyes, everything changed."

Suddenly, Caleb was no longer in his body. He was *everywhere*. He saw Earth being born. He saw himself as a healer in robes made of starlight. He saw children he had never met, but knew. He saw a woman with golden eyes whispering to him; "You are the key and the keeper. You are the return."

And then it all went dark.

Three hours later, he was found face-up in the snow by his climbing partners. No broken bones. No injuries. Just a faint symbol behind his ear - an eye within a ring. And a look in his eyes that no one could explain.

"I know it sounds impossible," he told me when we met. "But I didn't come back the same. I *can't* go back."

Since then, Caleb had become a conduit. He painted visions. He spoke languages he didn't know. He began receiving what he called *downloads* - messages about human evolution, quantum timelines, and the return of the ancient soul-tech we call the Spectacles.

Months later, he was led - by what he called "a pull in the chest" - to a small workshop where he heard about The Loveday Method for the first time.

He walked in, sceptical. He left trembling, activated.

"It had the same resonance. The same *hum* that filled the space I fell into. You've tapped into something real, Geoffrey. The Method… it's a tuning fork."

He later described the Loveday Method not as therapy, but as a "soul circuit reactivation."

A frequency. A remembering. A recalibration of all the lives he'd ever been - and would be again.

This is the mystery: the spectacles don't just return through lineage or grief. They sometimes arrive in moments that break the laws of physics - because *your soul doesn't obey those laws.*

Caleb didn't meditate his way to awakening. He fell - *literally* - into it. But when he landed, he remembered something that had always been there.

"The Spectacles aren't tools," he told me. "They're *living intelligence*. And once they touch you, you can't pretend the world is what it used to be."

You may never fall through the sky. You may never see glowing rings or hear the stars sing. But if you've ever had a moment of inexplicable clarity, felt time ripple in your hands, known something you shouldn't know, and dreamt of places that don't exist here - but feel more like home than anything you've known - then you, too, are remembering.

The spectacles are not fiction. They are *frequency*. And they're waiting for you to listen.

Chapter Thirteen: The One Who Didn't Believe

The soul doesn't need your belief. Only your attention.

Her name was Rowan.

She was logical. Brilliant. A science writer for a reputable journal, deeply grounded in evidence, research, and rationality. She came to one of my group workshops only because her friend bribed her with lunch afterward.

She arrived, arms folded, energy closed, but polite. She sat at the edge of the circle, as if proximity to spiritual conversation might infect her.

"I don't believe in past lives," she said quietly, more to herself than anyone. "But... I've been dreaming about someone else's life for over a year. And sometimes, when I wake up, I miss people I've never met. Places I've never been. And I don't know how to explain that."

That was the door. It was small. But it was open.

Throughout the day, Rowan didn't speak much. She took notes, eyes narrowed like she was collecting data. When we spoke about ancestral echoes, soul contracts, and energetic inheritance, she didn't react. But she didn't leave, either.

There was a stillness to her. A tension behind the eyes. Something *buzzing* just beneath the surface.

During a guided visualization, I watched her posture shift. A flicker across her brow. The faintest tremble in her fingers. Afterward, she avoided my gaze - but lingered after the group dispersed.

"Can I ask you something?" she said. "Have you ever remembered something that didn't belong to you... but broke your heart anyway?"

Rowan described a recurring vision. She was standing on a dirt path beside a sun-baked house with turquoise shutters. There was music coming from inside, laughter, the smell of jasmine. She wore sandals. Her hands were wrinkled, old. She was waiting for someone.

But they never came.

"I don't know where it is. Or who I am. But every time I wake up, I feel like I've just lost the love of my life. And the grief is unbearable. But it doesn't make sense. It's not *mine*."

She tried therapy. Journaling. Even hypnosis once. But nothing unlocked it.

Until The Loveday Method.

We worked together one-on-one after that day. With Rowan, there was no dramatic regression. No flood of visions. No screaming or shaking. Just breathe, stillness, soft questions. And space.

What began to unfold was *not* a memory from her own childhood. It was a life lived decades ago, in another country, by a woman named Soraya - a woman who had once waited for a lover who never returned from war.

"It was like watching someone else's ending," Rowan said. "But feeling it as my own."

And maybe it *was* her own. Maybe it was an echo from a past life. Or perhaps an ancestral thread passed silently down through her DNA.

But what mattered was what happened next.

After that session, Rowan began seeing patterns everywhere. Not mystical signs. But synchronicities were so precise, she could no longer dismiss them as coincidence.

She'd think of a name, and it would appear in the next article she edited. She'd dream of a place, then see a photo of it in a magazine. She began having conversations with strangers that felt like déjà vu - word for word.

"It's not that I suddenly believe everything," she admitted later. "It's just... I can't deny what I'm feeling. I *know* things now. I feel them before they happen. I remember things I've never experienced."

The spectacles had arrived.

Not through a crisis. Not through ceremony. But through the quiet collapsing of her own resistance.

Rowan taught me something vital. The spectacles aren't only for the seekers and the mystics. They find the sceptics too. They whisper to the doubters.

Because the truth doesn't need to be shouted. It just needs to be felt.

Rowan never called herself spiritual. She still doesn't. But when she speaks now, it's with the certainty of someone who has touched something beyond logic - and survived it.

"I don't know what I believe," she said once. "But I know what I've seen. And I know what I've remembered."

And sometimes, that's more honest than belief.

If you're reading this, and part of you is still unsure... still sceptical... still thinking, *"This sounds beautiful, but is it real?"...* you're not wrong for asking. You're not broken for not yet believing.

But if you've *felt* something - even just once - then the spectacles have already touched you. The remembering has already begun.

Chapter Fourteen: The Great Return

When enough souls remember, the whole world starts to awaken.

It didn't happen all at once. It never does.

The remembering began in fragments. A dream in Ireland. A vision in Kenya. A child speaking an ancient tongue in Tokyo. A woman drawing spiral symbols in the sand without knowing why in Peru.

Isolated events. Unexplained moments.

But slowly - across oceans, across timelines, across bloodlines - something began to synchronize.

The Spectacles were not returning to a few chosen people. They were returning to *everyone* who had ears to hear, eyes to see, and hearts brave enough to *feel again*.

One woman dreamed of a blue-robed healer standing in a forest with light pouring through his hands.

A week later, a man across the world began painting that same figure, weeping as the brush moved, unaware of why his hands were shaking.

A child in Canada started humming the melody of a song an elderly woman in Ethiopia had been hearing in her prayers for weeks - despite neither knowing the other existed.

Another man - who had never meditated in his life - fell into a spontaneous trance while folding laundry and began speaking a language his partner didn't recognise but felt in her bones.

These weren't random. They were *returned*. Reactivations of the same grid. The same soul-code. The same ancient remembrance is finally coming back online.

It wasn't just a method anymore. It was a frequency. A pulse.

People who had never heard of Geoffrey Loveday began describing the same energetic sensations. The same emotional surges. The same symbols. The same inner knowing.

"I don't know how I found this," they'd say. "But it feels like this found *me*."

The stories in this book had never been stories at all. They were blueprints. Mirrors. Signals. And now, the resonance was spreading like fire across dry fields.

The Ancients - the Rememberers, those who had offered the spectacles long before humanity had names for gods - watched.

Not with judgment. Not with intervention. But with joy.

"They are beginning," they whispered across dimensions. "The veil thins. The bridge is rebuilt."

Across the sky, dreams grew stranger. People began waking with languages they'd never studied. The space between synchronicities shrank.

And somewhere inside every soul... A memory bloomed.

It is not a revolution. It is not a religion. It is not even a movement. It is a *homecoming*.

A cellular reawakening of the truth we never truly lost - only buried.

It's the fire in Gema's yurt. It's Caleb's fall through the sky. It's the song Micah hummed beneath the stars. It's the ache in Shanna's back, the visions in Elliott's mind, the echo in Sarah's tears, the moment Rowan stopped needing to believe and simply *knew*.

If you're reading this, you're part of it.

You wouldn't be here if you weren't already feeling it. The dreams, the restlessness, the sense that something's coming, but it's also already here.

That's not anxiety. That's your soul waking up. That's the Spectacles adjusting over your inner vision. That's you stepping into your remembering.

You are not behind. You are not too late. You are not imagining things.

Chapter 15: The Sorrow in the Air

Have you ever paused and really felt it? The weight in the air. The depression that lingers, the quiet ache that seems to follow so many people through their days.

It's not just in the headlines. It's in the silence between conversations. It's in the children who can't sleep,
 in the teenagers placed on antidepressants at twelve

years old, in the adults who feel lost for reasons they can't explain.

Something is happening. And we're asking all the wrong questions.

Why now? Why this generation? Why, when the world seems more connected than ever, are we more disconnected inside?

Some will tell you its technology. Some will blame social media, pressure, or the chaos of the modern world.

But I believe the answer lies somewhere deeper. Somewhere older.

I believe we are feeling something we do not understand; the echoes of the past.

You see, years ago, depression wasn't something so openly seen. Of course, there was pain. There was grief. But not like this; this silent epidemic of sorrow.

What if what we are facing now isn't just ours? What if the anxiety, the heaviness, the depression so many carry are not just symptoms of modern life, but memories?

Memories from the lives lived before us. Emotions that were never released. Trauma that was never healed. Passed down not through stories, but through frequency. Through energy. Through the soul.

Like an invisible thread, these unresolved experiences travel across generations, whispering to us through emotion, illness, fear, and confusion.

And yet, we keep looking forward to the solution. More medication. More distraction. More noise. But the truth? The truth lies behind us.

Like a bridge, the past is calling; not to trap us, but to free us.

What if, instead of asking "What's wrong with me?" we asked, "What have I been carrying that was never mine to begin with?"

What if the sadness doesn't start with you, but with a child who lost everything three generations ago? What if the anxiety you feel isn't yours, but an echo from a soul once betrayed, now trying to find peace?

The mind forgets. But the body remembers. And the soul never lets go until it's ready to be seen.

This is where The Loveday Method comes in.

A way to step back. To return to the place where the wound first happened, whether that is in this life, or another.

To see it clearly, to feel it fully, and most importantly, to release it.

Because when you bring light to what was hidden, what once felt heavy begins to dissolve. You're not just healing yourself, you're healing the story. And changing the future.

So when I see a twelve-year-old placed on medication, my heart aches. Not because they are broken, but because they are carrying something too big, too old, and too silent for the world to notice.

But I see it. And maybe you do too.

That's why this work matters. That's why we must return to the beginning. To the echoes. To the root. Because if we can heal that, we can change this.

And if we teach the next generation how to remember, how to feel, how to let go, and how to truly come home to themselves, maybe, just maybe, they won't have to carry what we did.

And maybe they'll walk lighter. Maybe they'll dream bigger. Maybe they'll be free.

Chapter Sixteen: The Girl Who Couldn't Breathe

When Lily entered that memory, she wasn't simply imagining a story. She was *remembering*.

The soul does not forget. Not war, nor fear, nor the moment a child learns the cost of taking a single breath.

Lily didn't know this in her waking mind. But as she described the scene, the detail, the atmosphere, the weight of silence, I recognised it.

It was wartime Europe. Winter.

A time when entire cities lived under fear. When families disappeared in the night. When children learned too early how to hide.

Tomas was one of them. A child in occupied Poland, small, smart, and quiet. He had seen more by the time he was ten years old than most people see in a lifetime.

The memory Lily carried was of a single night.

Tomas had been hidden in a basement by his mother, beneath the old stone synagogue where his uncle worked. The air was damp and the floor was cold.

The soldiers had come unexpectedly; boots like thunder on the cobblestone streets. Windows shattered; doors splintered.

His mother had kissed his forehead and whispered, "Don't make a sound. No matter what." He obeyed. He always did.

Tomas sat in the darkness, arms wrapped around his knees. He could hear the soldiers barking orders, dragging people from their homes.

He heard his mother's voice, then a slap and a scream. Then silence.

He covered his mouth with both hands. Tears rolled down his cheeks and his lungs burned as he thought, "*If I breathe, they'll hear me.*"

That thought carved itself into him like a scar. That belief, so intense, so complete, became a command that reached beyond that life.

"Breathing is dangerous. To survive, you must be invisible."

When Tomas survived, when he was eventually found by resistance workers and smuggled across the border, he never spoke of that night.

But the fear never left. He grew up quiet, and avoided crowded places. He held his breath in arguments, in celebrations, even in moments of joy. It was buried. It stayed unspoken. Unprocessed.

And when Tomas passed on, his soul carried that unresolved fear forward into another life.

That life was Lily.

And though she was born in a peaceful country, in a safe home, the panic still found her.

It wasn't hers, but it lived in her body. It showed up in crowded classrooms, in sudden noises, in the moments where she couldn't catch her breath and didn't know why.

The world told her she had anxiety, but her soul was telling her something else; that long ago, she had learned it was safer not to breathe.

And now she was ready to unlearn it.

In our session, when she remembered Tomas, not as a character, but as *herself*, she gave voice to what had never been said.

She brought light to the dark. She returned to the moment of trauma, not to relive it, but to set it free.

And that is the quiet miracle of The Loveday Method. It doesn't invent stories. It helps souls remember the truth so they no longer have to carry it in silence.

Chapter Seventeen: The Seamstress of Silence

Not all pain comes from violence. Some comes from a life unlived, a voice never spoken, a dream that died in the dark.

Her name in this life was Maya. She was thirty-four, vibrant on the outside, but always apologising for things she hadn't done. Apologising for speaking, apologising for taking too long to make a decision, and apologising for simply existing too loudly.

She had come to me after years of therapy, years of learning the right words, but never really knowing where the ache began.

"I always feel like I'm in the way," she told me once. "Like I need permission just to be here."

She had a voice that wavered at the end of every sentence, as if asking the world, *"Is this okay? May I say this?"*

She wanted to understand why. She wanted to stop living like she was waiting for someone else's approval to breathe.

So we began.

As I guided Maya into The Loveday Method, her body stilled. Her breathing slowed, and the air around her seemed to soften, as if memory itself was preparing to return.

She climbed the inner staircase. She opened the door. And her voice changed.

"It's hot," she whispered. "And loud. So many people talking. Dust everywhere. Needles. Clothes."

She was standing in a small workshop, a sewing house in India, sometime in the late 1700s.

She was not Maya. She was Amara, a young woman, around eighteen. A gifted embroiderer known for her delicate hands and perfect stitches.

But no one knew her name. They knew her work, not her voice. Not her story.

She had been born into a caste that was never meant to speak, only to serve. Only to sew, to mend, to stitch the beauty of the world into garments she would never wear.

But Amara still had her own dreams. She wrote poetry when no one was looking. She sang songs under her breath. She had once spoken her ideas aloud to the son of a merchant and he had smiled, then told her never to do that again.

She learnt quickly that silence is safer. Silence is survival. And yet, her soul burned with words, ideas, and art.

But each time she opened her mouth, shame met her like a stone. "I had thoughts that were never heard," Maya whispered in the session. "Whole pieces of myself that lived only in my mind."

"No one ever asked me who I was. Only what I could make."

And then the pain came. Not sharp, but hollow, like a house filled with echoes of what was never said.

In this life, Maya had grown up in a world of education, rights, and opportunity. And still, she couldn't speak without shrinking. She couldn't share an idea without second-guessing it. She would write, then delete. Speak, then apologise. Dream, then disown it.

Now, she understood why.

Amara's voice had been buried, not by cruelty, but by expectation. By tradition. By invisibility. That silence had followed her across lifetimes.

Until now.

I guided her to stand in that small sewing room as Amara, but also as Maya.

And to speak. To say something that had never been heard.

Her voice trembled at first. But then it rose. She spoke words she didn't recognise, but somehow knew. A poem, perhaps. A truth.

And in the air around us, something shifted.

"I don't have to earn the right to speak," she said quietly,

tears falling freely. "I am allowed to take up space."

After the session, Maya didn't speak at first. But her posture had changed. Her shoulders were no longer caved. Her breath moved freely, deeper.

The next week, she stood in front of her colleagues and shared an idea she'd been holding back for months. They listened. And she didn't apologise.

She submitted a piece of writing to a magazine. She read her poetry aloud at a small open mic session. She stopped whispering.

Because what Amara could not do, Maya finally could. And that is what healing looks like, when the soul is ready.

Some wounds are loud. Others are silent. Some are caused by violence. Others by invisibility. But all of them deserve light.

And when we use The Loveday Method to trace those echoes, to the dusty sewing room, the stone hiding place, the silent ache, we don't just release the pain, we release the potential that was trapped beneath it.

The voice. The truth. The right to be seen.

Chapter Eighteen: The Soldier Who Never Spoke

Some echoes aren't loud. They don't arrive as screams or visions. They arrive in silence. And they stay until someone dares to listen.

His name was Daniel. Forty-two years old, strong, grounded, and reliable. The kind of man people leaned on. A quiet pillar in the background of other people's lives.

He wasn't one for deep conversations. He didn't complain. He didn't cry. But there was something always beneath the surface, a certain stillness that felt more like suppression than peace.

He came to me not because he believed in past lives or energy healing. He came because his daughter was struggling with crippling anxiety, and someone had suggested *The Loveday Method*.

But when we spoke, it became clear that the echo didn't begin with her.

Daniel told me about his father, a man who had served in the Second World War.

"He never talked about it," he said. "Never spoke a word of what he saw. But you could feel it in the house. He was never really... here."

Daniel grew up respecting silence. He learned early that emotions were a private matter. That pain was something men held quietly, like a shield inside the chest.

But now, watching his daughter struggle to breathe at night, feeling anxiety that seemed to appear from nowhere, he began to wonder; "What if we were carrying something we never chose? What if silence is not strength, but a wound passed down through the bloodline?

He agreed to try the method. Not for himself, he said. But for her.

As I guided him through the staircase, I noticed how calm his breath remained. How he controlled even his relaxation as if softening was something dangerous.

But when he reached the door and opened it, everything changed.

"It's raining," he whispered. "I'm cold. My feet are soaked. There's a rifle in my hands."

His voice thickened.

"There's shouting. Smoke. I can't tell where the front line is."

He paused. Then said, barely above a whisper, "I just saw my best friend die."

His body trembled slightly. A single tear fell, unwilled, unexpected.

"His name was Thomas. I held him until he stopped breathing. I didn't cry. I didn't scream. I just shut down."

He was a British soldier, somewhere in France, 1917. A young man in the trenches, surrounded by horror he had no words for. He did what every man around him did; he survived. And to survive, he turned off every feeling inside him.

"When I came home, people clapped and cheered. But I couldn't feel anything. I stopped talking. I stopped living."

That soldier never recovered from what he saw. He married, he raised children, and he worked a quiet job until the end of his days.

And in his silence, he unknowingly passed the wound down, through gestures, through unspoken fear, through the way he never hugged his son, through the way that son learned to never cry.

That son was Daniel's father.

And now, it lives in Daniel. And his daughter. A pattern woven not through genetics, but through soul memory.

In the session, Daniel wept. Not loudly. Not dramatically. Just the kind of tears that come from a dam finally cracking open after a century of holding too much.

He forgave the soldier. He forgave his father. And he forgave himself.

And he spoke, for the first time, the words that were never said; "You didn't fail. You were just trying to survive. But it's okay now. You don't have to carry it anymore. And neither do I."

Daniel didn't come back right away. But a month later, he emailed me; "My daughter's panic attacks have stopped. She still gets anxious sometimes - but she isn't afraid anymore. And I'm not afraid to feel. Something's changed. In me and in our home. Thank you."

Because sometimes, the healing doesn't begin in the person who's suffering. Sometimes, it begins in the one who chooses to go deeper. To break the chain. To finally say what no one before them could.

This is what it means to heal the inheritance. To meet the silence, and turn it into something sacred.

Chapter Nineteen: The One Who Almost Missed It

The call doesn't stop just because we stop answering.

Her name was Mariel.

She was seventy. Fierce, funny, and sharp as ever. But she spoke like someone who had packed up her dreams in a box and shoved them in the attic.

"I don't need to remember anything," she told me. "What's done is done. I've made peace with it."

But her eyes said something else.

There was a flicker behind them - like a candle that had burned for decades under a glass dome. Not out, but contained, controlled.

"I've lived through loss. Buried a child. Buried my mother. Watched the world change around me while I stood still. What good would remembering do now?"

She didn't come to awaken. She came because her granddaughter had been having visions.

Her granddaughter, Lena, was fifteen and wide open. Dreaming of people she'd never met. Speaking phrases in a language no one had taught her. Waking in tears from memories that didn't belong to her - but left stains on her heart.

"She says she feels things that make no sense," Mariel said. "That she sees me in different lifetimes. That she remembers my mother - even though she died before Lena was born."

I asked Mariel if she'd ever experienced anything like that herself. She paused, looked out the window, and then whispered: "Only every day for the past fifty years."

The remembering didn't come during a session. It came one night while Mariel was brushing her hair - alone in her home, late autumn wind tapping at the windows.

She looked up and caught her reflection in the mirror. Except it *wasn't* quite her. It was her face, but younger. Dressed in wool and linen, a red thread woven through her braid.

"I saw myself," she told me later. "But not here. Not now. I was in a stone room, writing something down, something I wasn't supposed to be writing."

And then, a wave of emotion hit her, but not sadness and not fear.

That night, she went to the attic. There, beneath a dusty trunk of childhood toys, was a journal she'd hidden in her twenties. Pages filled with automatic writings, visions she'd had and dismissed, names and dates she couldn't explain.

At the time, she thought she was losing her mind. She hadn't opened it in almost 50 years. But when she did, her hands shook. The ink had faded, but the messages were alive. One entry read:

"I will return to this. Not in this decade, maybe not in this life. But I will not forget forever."

And beneath it, in handwriting she didn't remember writing:

"Watch for the girl with the second sight. She will bring you home."

There was no fire. No trance. No regression. Just a soft unravelling. A letting go of disbelief. A quiet willingness to open the box she had sealed for decades.

Mariel didn't need to see visions. She *was* the vision.

All the memories she had stuffed away to protect herself were now blooming through her granddaughter. And instead of fear, she felt awe.

"It skipped me on purpose," she said, laughing softly. "But it found a way back. Through her. Through love."

Mariel began teaching Lena. Not formally, but through stories, through meals cooked from instinct, through walks in the woods where she finally shared the dreams that haunted her youth.

She no longer needed to remember *everything*. She just needed to stop running from it.

"I thought I missed my chance," she told me once, sitting in the sun, watching Lena gather herbs in the garden. "But the truth is - there is no 'too late' when the soul is ready."

Some awaken young. Some awaken through crisis. Some awaken in their final seasons. But all of us - every single one - will be called.

And whether we answer in this life or the next, the Spectacles will wait. Patient, ancient, and alive. Because the soul never forgets, even if we do.

A Soul Letter

From Geoffrey Loveday

Dear one,

If you're reading this, something in you has already remembered. Not a fact. Not a technique. But the truth.

A silent, soul-deep knowing that there is more to your life than what you've been told. More than pain. More than survival. More than carrying what was never meant to be yours.

You didn't find this book by accident. This isn't entertainment. This is a return.

A return to your own wisdom. A return to the places in your spirit that never forgot who you are. A return to the rhythm of healing that belongs not to any system or method, but to the Earth, to the breath, to the soul.

You don't need to do anything dramatic now. Just begin.

In small ways. In quiet mornings. In the space between your thoughts.

Notice what rises. Notice what repeats. Notice what feels too old for this lifetime.

That's where the remembering lives.

You may still doubt it. You may still ache. You may still wonder if you're making it all up. That's okay.

But I want you to know, *What you feel is real.* The things you're sensing, seeing, dreaming, grieving, they matter.

They are not madness. They are messages. You are not broken. You are *becoming*.

The spectacles are already with you. They live behind your eyes, in your breath, in your body's mysterious wisdom. You are not waiting for them to arrive. You are learning to see again.

And as you do, you awaken the world with you.

So take your time. But don't turn back. You've remembered too much to pretend otherwise. This is your path now.

You're not walking it alone. We're walking it together. And I am deeply, truly honoured to walk it beside you.

With love and presence,

Geoffrey Elliott Loveday,

Fellow Rememberer and Creator of

The Loveday Method

Chapter Twenty: The Thread of Time

This is not just a book. It is a doorway. A thread. A remembering.

You've walked through stories that defy logic. Lives lived in other centuries. Fears that were born long before the children that carried them. Gifts silenced across generations. Souls reaching out through time to be seen, to be heard, to be whole.

And yes - some of it may have seemed impossible, strange, and unbelievable.

But if you've made it here, to this page, this moment, this breath, then perhaps some part of you knows already that we are not just living one life. That the pain we carry is not always ours. And that our anxiety, our sorrow, our sense of not belonging, might be echoes of a story long unfinished.

The past is not behind us. It is *within* us. Like a golden thread running through every heartbeat, every emotion, every thought we can't quite explain.

It connects us to those who came before, and those who are yet to come. It is not a chain, it is a bridge.

And when we walk that bridge consciously, when we look back, not to suffer, but to understand, we begin to reclaim something sacred; our peace, our power, our true self.

The Loveday Method is not just a healing technique. It is a compass for the soul. A way to turn inward, not away. To step beyond time, not escape it. To listen to the quiet voice that says, *"You've been here before. And now, you are ready."*

Ready to release what was never yours. Ready to forgive what was carried too long. Ready to become the one who breaks the pattern, so the next generation doesn't have to carry it.

This is how we give them peace. Not by fixing the world outside, but by healing the world within.

When we remember, we release. When we release, we change. When we change, the future changes with us.

We are not broken. We are remembering. And through that remembering, we pass on something new; not pain, but freedom. Not fear, but truth. Not silence, but peace.

The journey never really ends. But it does deepen. And now, it is your turn to close your eyes; to walk the staircase; to find the door; and to listen to the soul that's been whispering all along, *"You are ready now. It's time to remember who you are."*

And when you do, you won't just heal yourself, you will heal everyone who came before you, and everyone who will come after.

This is the gift. This is the legacy. This is The Loveday Method.

A method. A memory. A return.

Thank you for walking this path. The Book remembers you. And now, you remember it.

The end is only the beginning.

We Have Reached the End of the Book

What Have You Learned?

If you're here, it means you stayed the course. You followed the threads. You walked through fire and memory, silence and vision, resistance and return.

So now, we ask, "What have you learned - not just in your mind, but in your bones?"

Have you noticed how grief speaks in dreams? How your body whisper what your ancestors never got to say? Have you remembered that your sadness might not be yours? That your strength has roots deeper than you imagined?

Have you seen how remembering doesn't always look like revelation, sometimes it looks like a sigh. A shift. A sudden understanding in the middle of an ordinary day.

Have you learned that you are not alone? That the journey of awakening is not a straight line, but a spiral? That the spectacles are not a fantasy, but a frequency?

That healing is not fixing, its *finding*?

More than anything, have you learned to trust yourself again? To trust what rises. To trust what returns. To trust that your story, however broken it may have felt, was never meant to end in silence.

You are the bridge. The echo. The remembering.

You are the fire starter and the flame keeper. The healer and the healed.

And this book? This was never just a collection of stories. This was your invitation to begin.

Before you go, ask yourself this: "What am I still carrying that I'm ready to put down? What part of me has returned? Who am I now that I've remembered?"

Then breathe, smile, and take one step forward.

Because the book may be finished - but your journey has just begun.

The Book of the Unknown, The Book of Echoes, The Enchanted Spectacles: What Is Real?

The book you are holding, or the story you are reading, was written in a different way, a way that invites you, the reader, to decide for yourself. The Book of the Unknown, the Book of Echoes, and the Enchanted Spectacles are not merely tales told through ink and paper. They are more than just the stories of Dorian,

Zasa, or anyone else. They are part of something deeper, something that transcends the ordinary bounds of time and space.

What if the stories are real? What if the Coat of a Thousand Lives, the Book of Echoes, and the Enchanted Spectacles are not just relics of the past, but possibilities woven into the fabric of our future? You, the reader, must decide what you believe. You must decide whether the power to heal, to move through time, and to understand the interconnectedness of the past, present, and future is a mere fantasy or a truth waiting to be unlocked.

We have always had the power to heal. Every culture, every people, has known this in some form: the power to mend not just the body, but the spirit, the mind, and the world. It's in the stories we tell, the rituals we perform, and the beliefs we carry.

For centuries, we have been taught to forget this power, to believe that healing is something only achieved through external means, through science and medicine alone. But what if it is much deeper than that?

What if the Book of the Unknown holds the answer, and the ability to heal is simply waiting for us to remember?

What if the Enchanted Spectacles are real? They allow the wearer to see beyond the veil of time, to feel what others have felt, to experience what was once thought impossible—seeing not just the past, but the future, and the emotions that lie hidden beneath the surface of every life lived. Could this be possible? Could we, through a shift in perception, connect with lives that have already been lived, or glimpse those that are yet to come?

The Book of Echoes, too, speaks of this connection, a connection that stretches through time. It whispers of lives interwoven, of people who are bound not by their physical existence, but by the invisible threads that run through all of us, binding our souls together in ways we cannot always see or understand.

Could the echoes of the past, the lives lived and lost, influence the choices we make today, or even shape the future we are yet to live? Is it possible that the stories contained in this book, and in every person we meet, have the power to guide us toward a future where healing, peace, and understanding are possible?

Time, in this context, is not linear. The past, the present, and the future are not separate entities, but part of a larger, interconnected whole. In this framework, the healing we seek is not limited by the restrictions of time.

To heal the present, we must first understand the past and the future—how they are intertwined, how they shape one another, and how our actions today influence the world we will live in tomorrow.

You, as the reader, are now part of this story. You are not just an observer—you are a participant. The power to heal, to move through time, to access the hidden truths within the Book of the Unknown and the Book of Echoes, is within you. The Enchanted Spectacles may not be a tangible object you can hold, but the ability to see beyond the surface, to understand the unseen, is something we all have within us.

But do you believe it? Do you believe that the Book of the Unknown holds the key to the healing of the world? That the power to change the course of history rests not in the hands of the few, but in the hearts of all of us?

The world is changing, and with it, the ways in which we understand ourselves, our past, and our future. Perhaps the time has come to remember what we have forgotten—to rediscover the power we have always had within us to heal ourselves, each other, and the world.

So, I leave it to you—the reader—to decide: What is real? Is it the stories told within these pages, or something deeper, hidden beneath the words? Can we heal through the mind, through time, and through understanding? Or is it all just a dream?

Only you can decide what is real, and in doing so, you might just unlock the truth of who we are, and who we are yet to become.

Dedication

To those who carry silent stories; may you one day find the words to speak them.

To the ones haunted by dreams not their own, you are not broken. You are remembering.

And to the forgotten: You were never truly lost.

This is for you.

Coming In 2026

The Crystal: A Touch Through Time

Fourth in the Series of Seven Books

The Origin of The Loveday Method®

A Heptalogy

By

Geoffrey Loveday

www.ingramcontent.com/pod-product-compliance
Lightning Source LLC
Chambersburg PA
CBHW071148070526
44584CB00019B/2710